ROSEMARY SUTCLIFF

BLACK SHIPS

BEFORE TROY

THE STORY OF **THE ILIAD**

F

FRANCES LINCOLN
CHILDREN'S BOOKS

BLACK
SHIPS
BEFORE
TROY

THE STORY OF THE ILIAD

Black Ships Before Troy copyright © Frances Lincoln Limited 1993
Text copyright © Anthony Lawton 1993

First published in Great Britain in 1993 by
Frances Lincoln Children's Books, 4 Torriano Mews,
Torriano Avenue, London NW5 2RZ
www.franceslincoln.com

This edition published in 2008

British Library Cataloguing in Publication Data
available on request

ISBN 978-1-84507-827-0

Set in Apollo and Baker Signet

Printed in the UK by CPI Bookmarque, Croydon, CR0 4TD

1 3 5 7 9 8 6 4 2

 # CONTENTS

IN THE HIGH and far-off days when men were heroes and walked with the gods, Peleus, king of the Myrmidons, took for his wife a sea nymph called Thetis, Thetis of the Silver Feet. Many guests came to their wedding feast, and among the mortal guests came all the gods of high Olympus.

But as they sat feasting, one who had not been invited was suddenly in their midst: Eris, the goddess of discord, had been left out because wherever she went she took trouble with her; yet here she was, all the same, and in her blackest mood, to avenge the insult.

All she did – it seemed a small thing – was to toss down on the table a golden apple. Then she breathed upon the guests once, and vanished away.

The apple lay gleaming among the piled fruits and the brimming wine cups; and bending close to look at it everyone could see the words 'To the fairest' traced on its side.

Then the three greatest of the goddesses each claimed that it was hers. Hera claimed it as wife to Zeus the All-father, and queen of all the gods. Athene claimed that she had the better right, for the beauty of wisdom such as hers surpassed all else. Aphrodite only smiled, and asked who had a better claim to beauty's prize than the goddess of beauty herself.

They fell to arguing among themselves; the argument became a quarrel, and the quarrel grew more and more bitter, and each called upon the assembled guests to judge between them. But the other guests refused, for they knew well enough that whichever goddess they chose to receive the golden apple, they would make enemies of the other two.

In the end, the three took the quarrel home with them to Olympus. The other gods took sides, some with one and some with another, and the ill will between them dragged on for a long while. More than long enough, in the world of men, for a child born when the quarrel first began to grow to manhood and become a warrior or a herdsman. But the immortal gods do not know time as mortals know it.

Now on the north-east coast of the Aegean Sea, there was a city of men. Troy was its name, a great city surrounded by strong walls, and standing on a hill hard by the shore. It had grown rich on the tolls that its kings demanded from merchant ships passing up the nearby straits to the Black Sea cornlands and down again. Priam, who was now king, was lord of wide realms and long-maned horses, and he had many sons about his hearth. And when the quarrel about the golden apple was still raw and new, a last son was born to him and his wife Queen Hecuba, and they called him Paris.

There should have been great rejoicing, but while

Hecuba still carried the babe within her, the soothsayers had foretold that she would give birth to a firebrand that should burn down Troy. And so, when he was born and named, the king bade a servant carry him out into the wilderness and leave him to die. The servant did as he was bid; but a herdsman searching for a missing calf found the babe and brought him up as his own.

The boy grew tall and strong and beautiful, the swiftest runner and the best archer in all the country around. So his boyhood passed among the oak woods and the high hill-pastures that rose towards Mount Ida. And there he met and fell in love with a wood nymph called Oenone, who loved him in return. She had the gift of being able to heal the wounds of mortal men, no matter how sorely they were hurt.

Among the oak woods they lived together and were happy – until one day the three jealous goddesses, still quarrelling about their golden apple, chanced to look down from Olympus, and saw the beautiful young man herding his cattle on the slopes of Mount Ida. They knew, for the gods know all things, that he was the son of Priam, king of Troy, though he himself did not know it yet; but the thought came to them that he would not know who they were, and therefore he would not be afraid to judge between them. They were growing somewhat weary of the argument by then.

So they tossed the apple down to him, and Paris put

up his hands and caught it. After it the three came down, landing before him so lightly that their feet did not bend the mountain grasses, and bade him choose between them, which was the fairest and had best right to the prize he held in his hand.

First Athene, in her gleaming armour, fixed him with sword-grey eyes and promised him supreme wisdom if he would name her.

Then Hera, in her royal robes as queen of heaven, promised him vast wealth and power and honour, if he awarded her the prize.

Lastly, Aphrodite drew near, her eyes as blue as deep-sea water, her hair like spun gold wreathed around her head, and, smiling honey-sweet, whispered that she would give him a wife as fair as herself, if he tossed the apple to her.

And Paris forgot the other two with their offers of wisdom and power, forgot also, for that moment, dark-haired Oenone in the shadowed oak woods; and he gave the golden apple to Aphrodite.

Then Athene and Hera were angry with him for refusing them the prize, just as the wedding guests had known that they would be; and both of them were angry with Aphrodite. But Aphrodite was well content, and set about keeping her promise to the herdsman who was a king's son.

She put a certain thought into the heads of some of King Priam's men, so that they came cattle-raiding at the full of the moon and drove off Paris' big beautiful herd-bull who was lord of all his cattle. Then Paris left the hills and came down into Troy, seeking his bull. And there Hecuba his mother chanced to see him, and knew by his likeness to his brothers and by something in her own heart that he was the son she had thought dead and lost to her in his babyhood. She wept for joy, and brought him before the king; and seeing him living and so good to look upon, all men forgot the prophecy, and Priam welcomed him into the family and gave him a house of his own, like each of the other Trojan princes.

There he lived whenever he would, but at other times he would be away back to the oak woods of Mount Ida, to his love Oenone.

And so things went on happily enough for a while.

But meantime, across the Aegean Sea, another wedding had taken place, the marriage of King Menelaus of Sparta to the Princess Helen, whom men called Helen of the Fair Cheeks, the most beautiful of all mortal women. Her beauty was famous throughout the kingdoms of Greece, and many kings and princes had wished to marry her, among them Odysseus whose kingdom was the rocky island of Ithaca.

Her father would have none of them, but gave her to Menelaus. Yet, because he feared trouble between her suitors at a later time, he caused them all to swear that they would stand with her husband for her sake, if ever he had need of them. And between Helen and Odysseus, who married her cousin Penelope and loved her well, there was a lasting friendship that stood her in good stead when she had sore need of a friend, years afterward.

Even beyond the furthest bounds of Greece, the fame of Helen's beauty travelled, until it came at last to Troy, as Aphrodite had known that it would. And Paris no sooner heard of her than he determined to go and see for himself if she was indeed as fair as men said. Oenone wept and begged him to stay with her; but he paid no heed, and his feet came no more up the track to her woodland cave. If Paris wanted a thing, then he must have it; so he begged a ship from his father, and he and his companions set out.

All the length of the Aegean Sea was before them, and the winds blew them often from their true course. But they came at last to their landfall, and ran the ship up the beach and climbed the long hill tracks that brought them to the fortress-palace of King Menelaus.

Slaves met them as they met all strangers in the outer court, and led them in to wash off the salt and the dust of the long journey. And presently, clad in fresh clothes, they were standing before the king in his great hall, where the fire burned on the raised hearth in the centre and the king's favourite hounds lay sprawled about his feet.

"Welcome to you, strangers," said Menelaus. "Tell

11

me now who you are and where you come from, and what brings you to my hall."

"I am a king's son, Paris by name, from Troy, far across the sea," Paris told him. "And I come because the wish is on me to see distant places, and the fame of Menelaus has reached our shores, as a great king and a generous host to strangers."

"Sit then, and eat, for you must be way-weary with such far travelling," said the king.

And when they were seated, meat and fruit, and wine in golden cups were brought in and set before them. And while they ate and talked with their host, telling the adventures of their journey, Helen the queen came in from the women's quarters, two of her maidens following, one carrying her baby daughter, one carrying her ivory spindle and distaff laden with wool of the deepest violet colour. And she sat down on the far side of the fire, the women's side, and began to spin. And as she span she listened to the stranger's tales of his journeying.

And in little snatched glances their eyes went to each other through the fronding hearth-smoke. And Paris saw that Menelaus' queen was fairer even than the stories told, golden as a corn-stalk and sweet as wild honey. And Helen saw, above all things, that the stranger prince was young. Menelaus had been her father's choice, not hers, and though their marriage was happy enough, he was much older than she was, with the first grey hairs already in his beard. There was no grey in the gold of Paris' beard, and his eyes were bright and there was laughter at the corners of his mouth. Her heart quickened as she looked at him, and once, still spinning, she snapped the violet thread.

For many days Paris and his companions remained the guests of King Menelaus, and soon it was not enough for Paris to look at the queen. Poor Oenone was quite forgotten, and he did not know how to go away leaving Helen of the Fair Cheeks behind.

So the days went by, and the prince and the queen walked together through the cool olive gardens and under the white-flowered almond trees of the palace; and he sat at her feet while she span her violet wool, and sang her the songs of his own people.

And then one day the king rode out hunting. Paris made an excuse not to ride with him, and he and his companions remained behind. And when they were alone together, walking in the silvery shade of the olives while his companions and her maidens amused themselves at a little distance, Paris told the queen that it was for sight of her that he had come so far, and that now he had seen her he loved her to his heart's core and could not live without her.

"You should not have told me this," said Helen. "For I am another man's wife. And because you have told me it will be the worse for me when you go away and must leave me behind."

"Honey-sweet," said Paris, "my ship is in the bay; come with me now, while the king your husband is away from home. For we belong together, you and I, like two slips of a vine sprung from the same stock."

And they talked together, on and on through the hot noontide with the crickets churring, he urging and she holding back. But he was Paris, who always got the things he wanted; and deep within her, her heart wanted the same thing.

And in the end she left her lord and her babe and her honour; and followed by his companions, with the maidens wailing and pleading behind them, he led her down the mountain paths and through the passes to his ship waiting on the seashore.

So Paris had the bride that Aphrodite had promised him, and from that came all the sorrows that followed after.

WHEN MENELAUS returned from hunting and found his queen fled with the Trojan prince, the black grief and the red rage came upon him, and he sent word of the wrong done to him and a furious call for aid to his brother, black-bearded Agamemnon who was High King over all the other kings of Greece.

And from golden Mycenae of the Lion Gate where Agamemnon sat in his great hall, the call went out for men and ships. To ancient Nestor of Pylos, to Thisbe where the wild doves croon, to rocky Pytho, to Ajax the mighty, Lord of Salamis, and Diomedes of the Loud War Cry whose land was Argos of the many horses, to the cunning Odysseus among the harsh hills of Ithaca, even far south to Idomeneus of Crete, and many more.

And from Crete and Argos and Ithaca, from the mainland and the islands, the black ships put to sea, as the kings gathered their men from the fields and the fishing and took up bows and spears for the keeping of their oath, to fetch back Helen of the Fair Cheeks and take vengeance upon Troy, whose prince had carried her away.

Agamemnon waited for them with his own ships in the harbour of Aulis; and when they had gathered to him there, the great fleet sailed for Troy.

But one of the war-leaders who should have been

15

with them was lacking, and this was the way of it. Before ever Paris was born, Thetis of the Silver Feet had given a son to King Peleus, and they called him Achilles. The gods had promised that if she dipped the babe in the Styx, which is one of the rivers of the underworld, the sacred water would proof him against death in battle. So, gladly she did as she was bidden, but dipping him headfirst in the dark and bitter flood, she held on to him by one foot. Thus her fingers, pressed about his heel, kept the waters from reaching that one spot. By the time she understood what she had done it was too late, for the thing could not be done again; so ever after she was afraid for her son, always afraid.

When he was old enough his father sent him to Thessaly, with an older boy, Patroclus, for his companion, to Chiron, the wisest of all the Centaurs. And with the other boy, Chiron taught him to ride (on his own back) and trained him in all the warrior skills of sword and spear and bow, and in making the music of the lyre, until the time came for him to return to his father's court.

But when the High King's summons went out and the black ships were launched for war, his mother sent him secretly to the Isle of Scyros, begging King Lycomedes to have him dressed as a maiden and hidden among his own daughters, so that he might be safe.

How it came about that Achilles agreed to this,

no one knows. Maybe she cast some kind of spell on him, for love's sake. But there he remained among the princesses, while the ships gathered in the world outside.

But Thetis' loving plan failed after all, for, following the sea-ways eastward, part of the fleet put in to take on fresh water at Scyros where the whisper was abroad that Prince Achilles was concealed.

King Lycomedes welcomed the warriors but denied all knowledge of the young prince. The leaders were desperate to find him, for Calchas, chief among the soothsayers who sailed with them, had said that they would not take Troy without him. Then Odysseus, who was not called the Resourceful for nothing, blackened his beard and eyebrows and put on the dress of a trader, turning his hair up under a seaman's red cap, and with a staff in one hand and a huge pack on his back went up to the palace.

When the girls heard that there was a trader in the palace forecourt, out from the women's quarters they all came running, Achilles among them, veiled like the rest, to see him undo his pack. And when he had done so, each of them chose what she liked best: a wreath of gold, a necklace of amber, a pair of turquoise earrings blue as the sky, a skirt of embroidered scarlet silk, until they came to the bottom of the pack. And at the bottom of the pack lay a great sword of bronze, the hilt studded with golden nails. Then the last of the girls, still closely veiled, who had held back as though waiting all the while, swooped forward and caught it up, as one well-used to the handling of such weapons. And at the familiar feel of it, the spell that his mother had set upon him dissolved away.

"This for me!" said Prince Achilles, pulling off his veil.

Then the kings and chieftains of the fleet greeted and rejoiced over him. They stripped off his girl's garments and dressed him in kilt and cloak as befitted a warrior, with his new sword slung at his side; and they sent him back to his father's court to claim the ships and the fighting men that were his by right, that he might add them to the fleet.

His mother wept over him, saying, "I had hoped to keep you safe for the love I bear you. But now it must be for you to choose. If you bide here with me, you shall live long and happy. If you go forth now with the fighting men, you will make for yourself a name that shall last while men tell stories round the fire, even to the ending of the world. But you will not live to see the first grey hair in your beard, and you will come home no more to your father's hall."

"Short life and long fame for me," said Achilles, fingering his sword.

So his father gave him fifty ships, fully manned, and Patroclus to go with him for his friend and sword-companion. And his mother, weeping still, armed him in his father's armour; glorious war-gear which Hephaestus, the smith of the gods, had made for him.

And he sailed to join the black ships on their way to Troy.

▦ QUARREL WITH THE HIGH KING ▦

THE GREEKS did not have smooth sailing. Storms beat them this way and that, and more than once they met with enemy fleets and had to fight them off. But at last they came in sight of the coast below Troy city.

Then they made a race of it, the rowers quickening the oar beat, thrusting their ships through the water, each eager to come first to land. The race was won by the ship of Prince Protesilaus, but as the prince sprang ashore an arrow from among the defenders took him in the throat and he dropped just above the tide-line, the first of the Greeks to come ashore, the first man to die in the long war for Troy.

The rest followed after him and quickly drove back the Trojan warriors, who were ill-prepared for so great an enemy war-host. And when that day's sun went down, they were masters of the coastwise dunes and reedbeds and rough grass that fringed the great plain of Troy.

They beached their ships, and built halls and huts in front of them to live in, so that in a while there was something like a seaport town. And in that town of turf and timber they lived while year after year of war went by.

Nine times the wild almonds flowered and fruited on the rocky slopes below the city. Nine times summer dried out the tamarisk scrub among the grave-mounds of long-dead kings. The ships' timbers rotted, and the high fierce hopes that the Greeks had brought with them grew weary and dull-edged.

They knew little of siege warfare. They did not seek to dig trenches round the city, nor to keep watch on the roads by which supplies and fighting men of allied countries might come in; nor did they try to break down the gates or scale the high walls. And the Trojans, ruled by an old king and a council of old men, remained for the most part within their city walls, or came out to skirmish only a little way outside them, though Hector, their war-leader and foremost among the king's sons, would have attacked and stormed the Greek camp if he had had his will.

But there were other, lesser cities along the coast that were easier prey; and the men of the black ships raided these and drove off their cattle for food and their horses for the chariots that they had built, and the fairest of their women for slaves.

On one of these raids for down the coast, when the almond trees were coming into flower for the tenth time, they captured and brought back two beautiful maidens, Chryseis and Briseis, among the spoils of war. Chryseis was given to Agamemnon, who as High King always received the richest of the plunder, while Briseis was awarded to Achilles who had led the raid.

Chryseis' father, who was a priest of Apollo,

the Sun God, followed after and came to the Greek camp begging for his daughter back again, and offering much gold for her ransom. But Agamemnon refused, and bade the old man be gone, with cruel insults. And there it seemed that the thing was ended.

But soon after, fever came upon the Greek camp. Many died, and the smoke of the death-fires hung day and night along the shore, and in despair the Greeks begged the soothsayer Calchas to tell them the cause of the evil. And Calchas watched the flight of birds and made patterns in the sand, and told them that Apollo, angry on behalf of his priest, was shooting arrows of pestilence into the camp from his silver bow; and that his anger would not be cooled until the maiden Chryseis was returned to her father.

On hearing this, Agamemnon fell into a great rage, and though the other leaders urged him to release the girl, he swore that if he did so, then he would have Briseis out from Achilles' hall in her place.

Then Achilles, who had grown to care for Briseis, would have drawn his sword to fight for her. But grey-eyed Athene, who was for the Greek because Aphrodite was for Paris and the Trojans, put it into his mind that no man might fight the High King, and that all manner of evils, from defeat in battle to bad harvests, would come of it if he did. Even so, a bitter quarrel flared between them, though wise old Nestor tried to make peace.

Achilles, who despite his youth was the proudest and hottest-hearted of all the Greek leaders, called Agamemnon a greedy coward with the face of a dog and the heart of a deer. "It is small part you play in the fighting, but you take other men's prizes from them when the fighting is over, robbing them of the reward and the honour that is rightfully theirs – for this one reason, that you have the power to do it, because you are the High King!"

"I am the High King!" agreed Agamemnon, his face blackening as though a storm cloud gathered over it. "I have the power, even as you say, and let you not forget it! Also, as High King I have the right, and let you not forget that either, you who are no more than a prince among other princes!"

The quarrel roared on, despite all that the other leaders could do to stop it. And in the end it was Achilles who had the final word.

"Lord Agamemnon, you have dishonoured me; and therefore now I swear on all the gods that I will fight for you no more! Nor will I take any part in this struggle against Troy until my honour is made good to me again!" And he strode out from the council-gathering and went back to his own part of the camp, his own hall and his own black ships; and all the men of his own country with him.

Then Agamemnon, in a black and silent rage, caused Chryseis to be put into one of his ships, and

cattle with her for a sacrifice to Apollo, and ordered
Odysseus to take command of the ship and return the
girl to her father. And as soon as the ship had sailed, he
sent his heralds to fetch Briseis from Achilles' hall and
bring her to his own.

Achilles made no more attempt to resist, and stood
by as though turned to stone while the girl was led
weeping away. But when she was gone, he went down
to the cold seashore and flung himself down upon the
tide-line and wept his heart away.

And his mother, Thetis of the Silver Feet, heard the
voice of his furious grief from her home in the crystal
palaces of the sea, and she came up through the waters
like a sea mist rising, no one seeing her except her son.
And she sat down beside him and stroked his hair and
his bowed shoulders and said, "What bitter grief is
this? Tell me the darkness that is in your heart."

So, chokingly, Achilles told her what she asked; and
in his grief and bitter fury, demanded that she go to
Zeus the Thunderer, chief of all the gods, and pray him
for a Trojan victory that should make the High King feel
the loss of his greatest captain and do him honour and
beg for his return.

Thetis promised that she would do as he asked. But
it could not be done at once, for the father of the gods
was absent about some matter in the far-most part of his
world, and it must wait for his return to Olympus.

So for twelve days Achilles remained by his ships,

waiting and brooding on his wrongs. And Odysseus, having returned Chryseis to her father with the proper sacrifices and prayers and purification, came again to the ship-strand, with the promise that Apollo was no longer set against them, and had lifted the plague-curse away.

But still Briseis wept in the hall of the High King, and Achilles sat among his ships, nursing his anger as though it were a red rose in his breast.

WHEN THE TWELFTH DAY came, Zeus the Thunderer was once again on the high crest of Olympus; and Thetis went to him, begging that he would bring about a victory for the Trojans, that the High King and all the Greek war-host might sorely feel the loss of Achilles her son from among their fighting ranks. And though he did not really wish to, Zeus gave her the promise that she asked.

The father of the gods considered long how the thing should best be done. And that night he sent a false dream to Agamemnon as he lay sleeping in his timber hall. The dream took the shape of wise old Nestor, who stood beside the High King's bed, and told him, "O King and lord of kings, make the war-host ready for battle. For if you attack Troy this coming day Zeus promises to you the victory, and only grief and loss to the Trojan people."

When Agamemnon woke and saw the grey dawn light standing in his doorway, he remembered his dream and was great with hope. But as the light strengthened he remembered that dreams can lie. He was always one whose moods swung him first one way and then the other. And when he rose, instead of donning his war-gear and ordering out his heralds with the call to arms, he put on his robe and mantle and took his sceptre of olive-wood bound with gold and summoned the kings and captains to hear his dream and advise him on it. His own doubts spread to the men listening to him, and there was no eager cry for battle, but only men looking doubtfully at each other.

Then the High King suggested a mad thing. He said that he would test the temper of the army. He would summon them all together and tell them that the siege had already dragged on too long, and the time had come when they should run their ships down into the water, and burn the camp behind them and set sail for Greece. If the warriors took him at his word, however, their leaders were to turn them back before they reached the ships, and he would try some means to put fresh heart into them.

But the siege had indeed dragged on too long. The warriors' hopes had sunk low, and they were weary for their own homes and their wives and children left too long behind. As soon as they heard what Agamemnon had to say, they rose up like a sea before the west wind and, shouting joyfully, made for the ships with the dust rolling up in a cloud behind them. And their captains as eager as all the rest.

Only Odysseus stood firm, shouting to the chieftains that the High King did but jest, and a shameful thing it would be to leave the siege now when they had spent so long upon it. Taking in his hand the royal sceptre to use as a staff, he turned cattle-dog and herded the warriors back to the gathering place. They returned at last, though in an ugly humour, puzzled and without heart. But only one of them protested, an ugly bandy-legged fellow called Thersites, who jumped out before the rest and began a jeering speech, insulting the leaders and telling the war-host to run away, for they were not worth following.

Odysseus, knowing that he must be silenced quickly and the mood of the war-host must be changed, took and beat him with the sceptre until the blood came and Thersites cried like a baby. Odysseus flung him down, laughing at the sight he made. Those nearest joined in the laughter, and the laughter spread out to the far-most fringes of the army where men did not know what they laughed at. The warriors hitched up their weapons and cheered Odysseus when he and white-haired Nestor bade them make ready for battle in the name of the High King.

So company by company, following their kings and chiefs and captains, the Greeks harnessed the captured horses to their chariots and swept out over the plain in great wheeling masses, like cranes sweeping in from distant lands to their own marshes at mating time.

And the Trojans, taking heart from the knowledge that Achilles had turned his back on the fighting, came pouring out from their city to meet them. For the first time in all the long years of the siege, the two great war-hosts came face to face.

They checked, fronting each other in two long menacing battle lines; and out from the Trojan mass, into the clear space between, swaggered Paris himself, a spotted panther-skin across his shoulder and in his hands two bronze-headed spears and his great bow. He shouted a challenge to the Greek lines: to any warrior who would come out and meet him in single combat.

Then Menelaus, the rightful husband of Helen, was glad as a lion is glad on his kill, and leapt from his chariot, his armour flashing in the sun. But Paris, seeing who came against him, felt his heart shrink within him, from shame as much as fear, and fell back into the ranks of the Trojan host behind him.

There Hector found him, and tongue-lashed him in scorn for his cowardice, and managed to drive something of courage into him again. And while the courage lasted, he offered a formal bargain to end the war one way or the other by fighting Menelaus. A fight to the death; and Helen, with all her jewels upon her, to be returned to her first husband and her own people, if he himself were killed; while if Menelaus died, she should remain with him and the Trojans, and the Greeks return without her over the sea-ways to the lands from which they came.

The Greeks agreed to this, and so that the thing might be acceptable to the gods, Hector sent back into Troy for two lambs for sacrifice. While they were brought, Paris put on borrowed armour, for he had not come armed for battle; gleaming breastplate and leg-guards, and great helmet with a high nodding horsehair crest. And throughout the mighty warhosts of Greece and Troy every man took off his own armour, for the sun grew hot, and settled down, leaning on his shield, to watch in comfort.

Meanwhile Helen, who was at home among her women and weaving a great purple cloak on her loom, heard of the coming fight between Paris and her marriage-lord. She left her weaving and flung a veil over her head and hurried to the roof of the nearest gate-tower. King Priam was there already, and some of his elders with him, looking out over the plain and the two great armies gathered there.

And seeing her come, the old men murmured among themselves that there had been no shame all this while in fighting to keep so fair a lady, but that now it would be a fine thing for Troy if she were to go back to her first lord and her own people.

But Priam, who had always been kind to her, saw her flinch at their words, and put out his hand to draw her to him. "Dear child," he said, "I do not blame you for what has come to pass. It is the will of the high gods that has brought this evil between your people and mine."

But Helen wept and said, "Always you have dealt gently with me; but I wish that I had died before I left my marriage-lord and my babe, shameless as I am, and came with Paris across the sea to bring so much sorrow upon us all!"

She would have covered her face and drawn back from the edge of the roof, but Priam held her at his side, asking her the name of this one and that among the Greek heroes, to turn her thoughts a little in another way. And so they remained for a while, side by side, looking down.

Below, in the open space between the armies, a rough altar had been set up. The two lambs were sacrificed, and a great oath was taken by the leaders of both sides, to abide by the outcome of the combat, whatever it might be. Then a square fighting-ground was marked off and, while the two champions stood facing each other, two wooden tablets, one marked for Paris and one for Menelaus, were put into a helmet and Hector shook them up to decide who should cast the first spear.

Paris' lot flew out on to the trampled ground. There was a deep breath from those near enough to see. "Paris! Paris has first throw!"

Paris drew back his spear and made his cast, but his spear point was blunted on the boss of Menelaus' shield, and fell uselessly away.

Then Menelaus cried out in a mighty voice to the father of the gods, "Great Zeus! Grant me my rightful vengeance on this man who did me foul wrong, even while he ate my salt and slept beneath my roof!"

And he in turn made his cast, with all the force of his wrongs behind it.

The spear point drove clean through Paris' shield and breastplate and gashed the fine stuff of his tunic, but did not so much as nick the skin beneath, for the Trojan flung himself sideways just in time. With a roar of fury Menelaus rushed upon him with his great sword upswung. But the blade, slashing at the bronze comb of his helmet, shattered into four pieces that span away, bright and blinking in the sunlight.

Menelaus threw the useless hilt aside and leapt upon Paris like a panther on its kill, grasped him by the horsehair crest and began to drag him back towards the Greek lines. But Aphrodite caused the helmet strap to burst apart under Paris' chin, so that Menelaus found himself suddenly with the great crested helmet empty in his hands.

He whirled about and flung it into the midst of his own warriors, but when he turned again to finish his enemy, the Trojan prince was nowhere to be seen. Aphrodite had flung a cloak of invisibility about him and swept him back to his own house, safe within the high palace courts of Priam his father.

While Menelaus went raging up and down, seeking his enemy, the warriors of the Greek host shouted for victory. For, by right of the bargain between them and the Trojans, Helen was now theirs again, and with her on board they could run their ships down from the tide-line and sail at long last for their homes.

Helen, with her hand in the old king's, still looking down from the roof of the Scaean gate-tower, thought the same.

But Aphrodite went to her there, no one else seeing her come save as a flicker in the air like the darting of a swallow, and told her, "Come now, back to your own house. Paris, your lord, is there in the great chamber and calling for you."

"Paris is no longer any lord of mine. That time is past and I will not go, for all his calling," Helen said.

But the goddess of love was not to be so easily refused, and her brow grew dark, for all her beauty. "That is proudly spoken. But take care that the love I have shown you until now does not turn to hate. It would be no hard thing to turn the hearts of Greeks as well as Trojans against you; and then, between the two, you might indeed find most cruelly the death that you have cried out for."

Then Helen was afraid. She pulled her veil across her face, and followed the goddess back to her house. In the high chamber Paris sat on the edge of the bed, unarmed and looking as though he had come from flutes and dancing rather than a fight, save for the red weal of the helmet strap on his neck.

And standing before him fierce and bitter, she said, "So you have come back from the fighting-ground. Hear now my greeting to you. It is this: that I wish you had died out there between the war-hosts, at the hand of my true marriage-lord, who is a better man than you will ever be!"

Paris got up and held out his arms. "Nay, honey-sweet, those are hard words to a man new back from battle. There will be other times between me and Menelaus. And meanwhile, do not be forgetting the love that I have given you all these years."

"Do not you be forgetting the sworn bargain that makes me wife to Menelaus again, and no longer woman of yours!" Helen flashed upon him, and would have turned away. But Aphrodite knew that if Helen of the Fair Cheeks went back to her own people, the long war would be over and Troy the loser. Her own promise to Paris would have gone wailing down the wind and she would look foolish in the eyes of all the gods and have to bear the mockery of Hera and Athene. She cast her magic upon Helen so that she saw him standing there with his arms held out, as he had stood ten years ago among the Spartan olive trees with his ship waiting in the harbour.

And bitterly, but not able to help herself, she went into his arms again, and remained with him in the high chamber in Troy.

THE WAR might have ended that day, even so, for the truce still held between the war-hosts and made a breathing space in which men might have talked peace with each other. But Athene, on the side of the Greeks, determined that the truce must be broken. She put it into the head of Pandarus, one of the princes among Troy's allies, that it would be a fine and valiant thingto shoot down Menelaus and so be done with one of the foremost of the Greek leaders. So Pandarus nocked an arrow to his great horn bow, and drew and loosed, and the arrow thrummed on its way and drove through the king's breastplate, and drew the red blood.

When Agamemnon heard that his brother was wounded, he cried out that if Menelaus died, the army would lose heart and return home, and the Trojans would dance for joy on his grave.

Menelaus quieted him as though he were a startled horse. "Nay, do not be putting fear into the war-host. See, the arrow has not gone deep, and will come out with little harm done."

And so it was proved when Machaon, the healer to the Greek war-host, came to draw forth the barb.

Nevertheless, the truce had been broken and men were putting their armour on again; and the horns sounded for battle, the first full battle in all the long years of the war.

The two great war-hosts broke forward across the open space between, the Trojans and their allies loud as a flock of birds, shouting in all their different tongues, the Greeks in grim and deadly silence. They charged together, crashing shield against shield, as when mountain torrents coming down in spate rush together and set the crags ringing and echoing. This way and that the battle lines swayed as thrust answered thrust, and the long ranks began to separate into whirlpools and back-eddies such as form when the torrents meet, each eddy a smaller battle of its own in which men fought each other, eye to eye and blade to blade, on foot or from chariots.

And where a man fell, there a struggle would gather about him as the enemy strove to drag his body aside and strip him of the armour that was theirs by right of conquest, and his friends stood over him, fighting to keep his body from dishonour. The dust rolled up so that both war-hosts were parched and whitened with it; and men went down before the flights of arrows and throw-stones that came upon them from all sides.

Through it all, Diomedes of the Loud War Cry, with his battle drunkenness upon him, went raging up and down the plain, leaving dead men behind him as a flooded river leaves the torn-off limbs of trees.

Pandarus loosed one of his deadly arrows against him as he swept by; but, though it took him in the shoulder, it did no deeper harm than the shaft that he had loosed at Menelaus. And when Diomedes had called a friend to pull out the barb, he turned back on Pandarus with a mighty spear-cast that took him full in the face and sent him sprawling into dust and darkness.

This way and that the battle flowed as Hector, with Sarpedon, lord of the Lycians, at his side, forced the Greeks back almost to their ships, only to be swept back in their turn by Odysseus and Diomedes. But as the red day wore on, the tide of battle began to run more and more strongly for the Greeks and against the Trojans and their allies, until the war-hosts of Troy were fighting desperately with their backs almost to the city gates.

Then the foremost of the Trojan soothsayers came to Hector, where he stood at the bloody heart of things, and bade him leave his command to Aeneas and go back within the city to his mother the queen.

"Bid her gather her women," said the soothsayer, "and take the most splendid of all her jewelled robes, and go up to the temple of grey-eyed Athene and lay it across the knees of the sacred statue. And pray to Athene to cease from giving all her strength to the Greeks and show mercy to the people of Troy, who are her people also."

So, unwillingly, Hector left Aeneas in command and

strode back to the city gate. And as he went, the rim of his great oxhide shield kept knocking against his heels and the back of his neck at every step, as though it would hurry him on his way.

Inside the city he went straight to the royal palace of his father, King Priam, in the high citadel. His mother met him in the gateway with a brimming wine cup in her hands, and would have had him drink and pour an offering to the gods.

But Hector told her gently enough, "Nay, my mother, I am filthy from the battlefields, my hands too fouled to be pouring offerings to the gods. I bring you a message from the lookers into dark places, and when it is given I must be away back to the fighting without delay."

And when he had repeated to her the words of the soothsayer, he took his leave of her and went his way. But he did not at once return to the battle. First he went across the palace courts to the house that their father the king had built for his brother Paris, thinking to speak a few words with Helen for kindness' sake.

There, in the high chamber, he found his brother fussing over his armour and playing with his great bow, like a girl making ready for a party, instead of arming himself for the war-host. And at the far end of the room Helen was working with her maidens at a rich tapestry on the loom. Her back was to him and all the air in the chamber hummed with anger.

Standing in the doorway. Hector spoke to his brother. "Under the city walls men are dying because of the evil that you wrought ten years ago! Up now, leave this playing with your weapons as though they were toys. Get your armour on and join them!"

Paris smiled at him, the smile that so often turned away men's wrath, and getting up, reached for his breastplate. "My brother, there is justice in your harsh words. But it is not cowardice that has held me here — grief for my ill-doing has made me weak, and I was only seeking a few breaths of time to gather my strength before going out again among my sword-companions. All that you say, Helen has but now been saying to me and, behold, you find me in the act of putting on my war-gear."

Helen said without turning round, "If the gods were kinder, I would not find myself bound to one who must be urged to battle by his woman." Then she got up and swept coloured wools from the stool beside her, and bade Hector sit for a while.

But Hector shook his head. "I go now to take leave of my wife, and have little enough time for that. Get this fellow armed and roused for action, and maybe he will catch up with me before I leave the city."

And out he strode to his own house. But Andromache his wife was not there. Her maidens told him that, hearing of the Trojans driven back and the Greeks near to victory, she had gone running to the Scaean Gate like a wild thing, and the nurse with her, carrying their baby.

And there, following them, Hector found her on the roof of the gate-tower, with the babe Astyanax cuddled in his nurse's arms.

Andromache came running to him and caught his hand, weeping and begging him not to go back into battle. "If you go back, it is your death and you will not return to us again!"

"Like enough," Hector said. "That is why I have come to say goodbye."

At this she wept yet more wildly. "I have no father nor yet a mother, and my seven brothers went down to the dark kingdom of Hades all on the same day. But you have been father and mother and brothers to me, as well as my beloved husband; and now it seems that I must lose you all! Have pity on me and on our baby son! You have fought enough; bide now with us –"

Hector shook his head, and the high horsehair crest of his helmet tossed sideways on the wind along the battlements. "I cannot bide here with you, for there is another fate upon me. It is not that I love you too little – oh no, never that. I know in my heart that the time comes when Troy will be laid low and all my father's people; but my grief for that is less than my grief for you who, when that day dawns, will be carried away captive to weave at the loom in some stranger-woman's house and carry water in slavery from a foreign well. May I be dead by then and the earth heaped over me, that I may not hear them carry you away."

He reached out to take his little son in his arms, but the babe shrank back, scared by the great bronze helmet with its nodding horsehair crest. Hector laughed then, and Andromache with him for all her grief. He took off the frightening helmet and set it on the ground. Then Astyanax went to him happily. Hector dandled him in his arms and kissed him, and prayed aloud to the gods for the boy's future. Then he gave him back to Andromache, his arms for the moment around them both, holding as though he did not know how to let them go. "Dear, cease the weeping. Go back to your women and set them to women's work. War is the work for men."

And he picked up his helmet and went his way.

PARIS CAUGHT UP with his brother, and they went down from the Scaean Gate together as though there had been no hard words between them, and plunged back into the fight.

At their coming the Trojans took fresh heart and rallied. Once again the battle surged outward from the walls of Troy, and the Greeks were driven back and back, almost to the black ships. And so terrible was the slaying among them that Athene, seeing the slaughter as she looked down from the peaks of Olympus, paid no heed to the jewelled robe newly laid across the knees of her statue in the great temple of the high city of Troy. She determined to stop the fighting for what remained of that day.

So she put the thought into Hector's mind that, before the sun went down, he should end the day with another challenge to single combat, like the one with which his brother Paris had begun it; but one which should not end in confusion as the other had done. He called off his men from the chase, sending word by his heralds to Agamemnon. When both sides were again seated on the ground he issued his challenge, bidding the Greeks to send out a champion of their own choice against him.

Menelaus stepped out to take up the challenge for

the second time that day. But the High King would not allow it, knowing that his brother would stand no chance against the mighty Hector. So, once again, they drew lots out of a helmet, and this time the lot fell to Ajax of Salamis, tallest and strongest of all the Greek war-host.

For the second time that day the square fighting-ground was marked out and into it, to meet Hector, strode Ajax, blazing bright as the god of war himself, and carrying his great shield made of seven oxhides behind a layer of bronze. They taunted each other after the manner of champions about to fight, and then betook them to their spears.

Hector made the first cast, and his spear went through the bronze and through six oxhides until the seventh held it. Then Ajax threw in answer, and his point went through shield and worked breastplate, but did no other harm, for Hector had leapt sideways on the moment. Both men dragged out the throw-spears and flung themselves upon each other, stabbing with their spears shortened.

Ajax's blade caught Hector on the side of the neck so that the dark blood welled out. Hector's spear rang on the boss of Ajax's shield and the point was turned. He flung it aside and caught up a black and jagged stone lying nearby, and crashed it upon the shield, but Ajax sprang back and, heaving up a yet bigger stone, hurled it with all his strength against Hector, smashing the shield in on him, taking the strength from his knees and flinging him over on to his back.

Hector's world darkened and swam, but he scrambled gasping to his feet, his hand going for his sword. Ajax's sword was also out, and in a moment more they would have been close locked, blade to blade, but heralds from both armies came running and thrust their staves between them and bade them cease, for both had proved themselves worthy champions, and the night was coming on.

Leaning on his sword, with the sunset dazzling his eyes, Hector agreed to their command. "Let us stop the fighting for this day. We shall fight on afterward until the gods send one of us the victory. But now the day ends, and it is good to give way to the night."

"I am content to do as you say," Ajax replied; and they looked at each other without hatred.

Then Hector said, "Maybe we shall not meet again in battle; therefore let us part with an exchange of gifts, that people may say of us in time to come, 'Those two fought as enemies, but when they parted they were joined in friendship'."

He sent for a sword with silver-work on the hilt and gave it to Ajax; and Ajax gave him in return a broad belt, rich with purple. And so they parted and went back each to his own side.

And night came seeping among the ancient grave-mounds and the tamarisk scrub.

Next day there was a truce between the armies while both Greeks and Trojans gathered and burned their dead on great pyres across the plain. And in the night and day that followed, the Greeks built a wall of turf and stakes all along the landward side of their camp, with a ditch before it deep and broad enough to overset any chariot that tried to cross it, and strong gates with shooting-towers on either side.

With the first daylight the fighting began again, and all that fierce and weary day it surged to and fro. Twice, Hector's charioteer was killed beside him and twice he found a new driver for his raging horses and went plunging on, slaying as he went.

Once, Diomedes would have swept the Greek charge to the very gates of Troy. But Zeus, the lord of all the gods, saw him and gathered his rolling storm clouds, and out of the middle of them loosed crashing thunder and a wild lightning bolt that struck the ground in front of Diomedes' galloping horses. The flame-flare and the stench of burning sulphur made them shy, casting those behind them into confusion and so breaking the force of the charge.

By the day's end the Greeks were back to their bank and ditch again, with nothing but their ships and the tide-line behind them, and despair tightening on their hearts.

That night, for the first time, the Trojans did not retreat within the safety of their walls, but unyoked and tethered their horses, and sent into the city for wine and food. They built great fires on the plain, as many fires as there are stars in the sky, and fifty men encamped round each, eating and drinking and listening to the music of flutes, while the horses munched white barley fodder. And there they remained, waiting for the dawn that would surely bring them victory.

Meanwhile in the Greek camp, Agamemnon, in black despond, summoned a meeting of the leaders. He told them, in grim earnest this time, that since Zeus the Thunderer had set his face so utterly against them, he saw nothing for them but to burn their camp and launch their ships under cover of night and sail for their own land, giving up all thought of Helen and the conquering of Troy.

But Diomedes stood up and said, loud enough for the whole camp to hear, "Let the High King sail home if he has not the heart to remain here. The rest of us will remain until we have taken Troy town!"

The first time the High King had spoken to them of abandoning the siege, the blood of the war-host had been cold and weary, but now the bitter brightness of battle flared within them and changed all that. They were not for leaving the thing unfinished, nor for shaming their comrades who had died in the fighting. And the warriors set up a great shouting that they were with Diomedes and would fight on until the thing that they had come to do was done.

And the ancient King Nestor, always the wisest of the council, got up in their midst and said that the time had come when they must seek at all costs to win back Achilles to fight in their ranks once more. Let Agamemnon the High King send an embassy to his hall and promise to return the girl Briseis and make him rich gifts of gold and horses, and ask his pardon for the past insult.

"For," said the old man, "if he returns to fight among us, the Trojans, hearing of it, will lose heart almost before he mounts into his chariot, and we shall drive them back within their walls and hold them penned as we used to do. Or better still, cut them off and harvest them as men harvest a field of corn, so that never again will they come to their own gates."

Agamemnon pulled at the black jut of his beard, and his brows drew together. But in the end he admitted the wisdom of Nestor's words.

And so in a short while Odysseus and Ajax, who were among the closest of Achilles' friends, and old wise Phoenix, who had been his tutor before ever he went to Chiron in the mountains of Thessaly, set out for the place at the far end of the camp where his black ships were drawn ashore. And there they found Achilles sitting in the doorway of his turf-thatched hall, playing idly on his lyre with the silver crosspiece, and Patroclus at a little distance, polishing his helmet and listening with a troubled face to the music that he made.

Achilles leapt up to welcome them when he saw them coming. He asked Patroclus to bring food and wine, and in a while they were feasting together as though there was no trouble between them in all the world.

And when the feasting was over, Odysseus, speaking for the rest, told Achilles the reason for their coming: that they brought the High King's humble plea for pardon for the insult and the injustice done to him, and his promise to return the girl Briseis, and with her, rich honour-gifts of gold and horses and slaves. The promise, too, of wide lands and his own daughter in marriage when they came again to their own countries. All this, if Achilles would but leave his anger and come again to his place among them in the battle-mass.

Patroclus, standing nearby, listened with hope brightening in his face; but Achilles had nursed his anger so long and allowed it to drive so deep within him that now he could not let it go, even if he would.

When Odysseus had done speaking he said only, "Very splendid are the promises of the High King. But what reason has he ever given me to trust his promises, that because of them I should put my life, which is the only life I have, and sweet to me, in black peril? I had rather run my ships down into the water and sail homeward on the morning tide, than follow such a king as he!" And he kicked at a spitting pine log that had rolled half out of the fire. "I care nothing for the High King's gifts, and if ever the time comes, I will win for myself a wife of my own choosing."

Then Phoenix spoke up, and the old man was near to tears. "When you were a child, I tried to teach you to be a man great enough to master your own anger, and to forgive when the time came for forgiving. Until now, with the wrong against you still unrighted, it was proper that you should hold to your anger, indeed, honour demanded it. But now the High King is ready to make amends; now he asks your forgiveness and sends words of peace to you by men who are your dearest friends. Now the time has come to lay your anger by, and return to your comrades in their desperate need."

And Ajax added his own word (maybe it would have been better if he had not), saying that all this was because of one girl, and the High King was ready to give her back, and all else beside.

But Achilles said only, "Ajax, Odysseus, Phoenix, my friends, go back to Agamemnon and tell him this: I will not fight until great Hector sweeps the Trojan charge right to the prows of my own black galleys. Then, and only then, I will give him work for his spears!"

And with that for his last word, the embassy had to go back along the shorewise camp to the hall of Agamemnon the High King.

THE HORSES OF KING RHESUS

THERE WAS LITTLE enough sleep for any of the Greek leaders that night, none at all for Agamemnon. Too restless to stay within his own hall, he flung the lion-skin rug from his bed about his shoulders and went out, thinking to seek out wise old Nestor. But Menelaus also was awake and restless, and only a little way beyond the ships the two of them chanced upon each other, and stood together for a while gazing across the plain to the watch-fires of the Trojan war-host.

"A fine thing it would be," Menelaus said at last, "if one of our young men, lacking sleep like ourselves, were to make his secret way over to the Trojan camp and listen to the talk around the fires, and bring us word of what to expect when dawn comes and the fighting light returns."

The High King was much struck with this. "A fine thing indeed, and we will bring it about, my brother. But first we must put it to the council."

So they went and roused out old Nestor and the other chiefs, who did not wait to put on their armour, but flung about them the skin rugs from their beds and came just as they were.

First they visited the young warriors guarding the ship-wall, to be sure that they also were wakeful, and then they crossed the ditch and set themselves down where they had a clear view of the Trojan watch-fires, to discuss the plan.

Nestor said, "Let one of the young men go out in the darkness, into the Trojan camp, and either seek to capture for us a straggler whom we can question, or overhear the talk about the Trojan watch-fires. So we may learn whether they mean to remain in the open and maybe attack our camp at dawn, or go back again within their walls now that it must seem to them that they have worsted us."

Diomedes was on his feet almost before the old king had finished speaking. "That is a task for two men rather than one. I will go, if I may take another of my own choosing with me."

"Choose, then," said the kings and captains.

And he chose Odysseus.

Odysseus got more slowly to his feet. "Better be on our way, for the night is more than half gone."

They borrowed weapons from the young men of the guard, and leather helmets which would not catch the firelight as bronze would do, having hurried to answer the High King's summons unarmed. And they set out, prowling like a pair of hunting lions through the darkness and the scattered bodies of the dead.

At the very same time, in the Trojan camp, Hector had gathered together his own captains, and called for a man to enter the Greek camp and find out if the Greeks kept their usual watch, or if they were too weary, and so might be taken sleeping by a dawn attack. And to any man who would go out and bring back word of this, he promised the two best horses in the enemy camp.

Now among the Trojans there was a young man called Dolon, ugly and rather foolish, but very swift of foot, who cared for horses more than for anything else in the world. And he spoke up. "Great Hector, give me the chariot horses of Achilles, and I will pierce right through the Greek camp to the hall of Agamemnon himself, and bring you back the word you seek."

And he took his bow and flung a grey wolfskin over his shoulders and set out, running low, for the camp along the shore.

But Diomedes and Odysseus on their own hunting trail saw him coming, and guessed his purpose, and lay down among the dead of yesterday's fighting, until he was well past them. Then they sprang up and went after him like hunting dogs after a hare. Dolon heard their feet behind him and lengthened his stride. But he could not pull away from them, nor swing back to his own people, for the two men were too close behind.

So they ran him down just before he came to the ship-wall, and brought him to a stand, his teeth chattering in his head with fear as they grasped his arms. He broke into tears, begging them not to kill him, for he was the son of a rich man who would ransom him with much gold.

"Before we talk of ransom, tell us what you are doing here, so far from your own camp, so close to ours," Odysseus said.

And Dolon told how Hector had promised him the chariot horses of Achilles for spying on the Greeks.

"You aim high!" Odysseus said, smiling in the dark. "The horses of Achilles are not of mortal breed, and none may drive them save Achilles himself or the man he bids to drive them. But nonetheless it is well that we meet here, for now you shall tell us: do the Trojans plan to camp out here on the open plain to attack us at dawn, or to draw back within their walls, now that seemingly they have had the better of the fighting? And how are the Trojan guard-posts set? And where does Hector sleep this night, and where are his horses?"

For the thought came to him (his grandfather had been a famous thief, and the gift had come down to him) that it would be a thing worth the doing, to steal the best horses in the Trojan war-host.

And hoping to save his neck, Dolon gabbled forth all that Odysseus asked: that Hector was not sleeping, but with the council; that the Trojans kept their watches unsleeping, having their own people in the city to think of, but that their allies from other lands, their wives and children being safe at home, were not so careful; that whether or no there was a dawn attack depended on the word that he, Dolon, brought back from his spying.

"But if it is horses that you want," said he, "the best and most noble in all the camp are those of Rhesus, king of the Thracians, who came in to join us only this day. They lie at the eastern end of the camp. Big horses, wind-swift and white as swans, and with them his chariot, decked with gold and silver, fit for the gods."

Then he fell again to weeping and praying for his life. But Diomedes said, "That you may escape and return to spy on us again?" And he struck Dolon cleanly with his sword, so that his head fell from his shoulders while he was still pleading.

"So much for our straggler," Odysseus said. "Next, for the Thracian king's horses."

Quickly they covered the spy's body with reeds and young tamarisk branches, and, taking his bow and his marten-skin cap, set them high in the nearby tamarisk bush to mark the spot that they might not miss it on their way back. And they went on through the night.

They came to the Thracian camp and found no watch set and the warriors all sleeping deeply, King Rhesus in their midst beside his chariot with the twelve hearth-companions of his bodyguard all about him.

Diomedes slew the king and his twelve companions swiftly and in silence, making no sound to rouse the rest of the camp; and Odysseus dragged the dead men aside to make a clear path, that the king's horses, which had maybe never been in battle before, might not be frightened at being led out over the bodies of the slain.

Then they freed the straps by which the horses were tethered to the ivory chariot rail. They did not wait to take the chariot itself, splendid though it was, for night was wearing on towards dawn and already the rest of the camp was stirring. But leaping upon the horses' broad white backs, they urged them out, past the Thracians, dead or half-roused or still sleeping, and headed back for the ship-wall and their own camp, checking to gather up the weapons and the marten-skin cap of the wretched Dolon on the way.

Great was the welcome they received from the kings and leaders, and great the rejoicing at the tale they had to tell. For, with King Rhesus dead, it was sure that the Thracians would now go home, and so thousands of fresh warriors would be lost to the Trojans' war-host.

Then Diomedes picketed the horses beside his own and gave them a feed of the same honeyed wheat, while Odysseus stowed the bloody cap and weapons in the stern of his ship, ready to be dedicated to Athene. And when that was done, the two champions waded into the sea and bathed off the blood and the thick sweat of that night's work from their arms and necks and thighs. Then they scrubbed themselves in tubs of water made hot for them by the slaves until they felt themselves clean once more, and went to claim their share of the morning food and wine, for by that time dawn was well up the sky.

 # RED RAIN

DAWN WAS INDEED well up the sky, but over the Greek camp there was little light, for Zeus had spread a churning mass of black cloud across the sky above them; though where the Trojans gathered on the higher ground the sky was clear and the light strong. And soon, from the menacing cloud roof rain began to fall: rain that was as red as blood.

But despite the evil omen, the Greeks were of better cheer than they had been last evening, for Diomedes and Odysseus had put fresh heart into them. Agamemnon their High King put on his armour with a good heart, and drew up his front-fighters on foot with their chariots ranked behind to support them; and behind again, the spear-warriors, and the bowmen and slingers on the wings.

When the Trojans came rushing down they charged to meet them. The two war-hosts crashed together, cutting each other down as reapers cut their way through a field of corn. Soon the helmets of the bravest Trojans shone deep in the ranks of the Greeks, and Greek swords were slashing and stabbing deep among the Trojans. And all the while the over-arching arrows fell like a dark and hissing rain.

At noon, the drowsy time when shepherds in the hills make no noise for fear of rousing goat-legged Pan,

Agamemnon led the front-fighters in a savage charge. With his own hand he slew many chiefs in that charge, two of Hector's brothers among them. A great and terrible charge, in which foot-soldiers slew foot-soldiers and chariot men slew chariot men, and they broke into the Trojan mass as fire falls on a forest on a windy day, leaping and racing from tree to tree. Driverless horses crashed here and there, dragging empty and broken chariots behind them, and before their onslaught the Trojans fell back and back until they were close before the city gates. And there, under Hector's orders, they checked and re-formed their broken lines and drew breath to face the next charge of the oncoming Greeks.

But that charge broke before it reached them, for Agamemnon had taken a spear-gash in the arm, and the wound bled so much that he must needs climb into his chariot and be driven back to the ships for tending.

And Hector, seeing this, shouted the war cry like a huntsman crying on his hounds against a lion, and rushed forward at the head of his warriors, scattering the Greeks like spray. Indeed, he would have driven them back to the ships again in one great thrust, but Odysseus and Diomedes stood firm amid the rout, slaying all about them. Four of the Trojan chieftains went down to the thrusting of their mighty spears, and the Greeks took heart again and rallied. As Hector loosed the next battle-rush against them, Diomedes caught him a great blow on the helmet, which, though it did not pierce the shining bronze, sent him crashing to the ground.

His warriors closed about him with their shields, and in a few heartbeats of time he was up, the light coming back into his eyes. He sprang into his chariot and the charioteer whipped up the team as they headed away for the left wing of the Greek war-host.

Diomedes fought on where he stood until Paris, keeping as usual to the fringe of the battle, saw his chance and loosed an arrow that took him cleanly through the foot and pinned it to the ground. And when he had pulled out the arrow, Odysseus covering him with his great shield the while, it was his turn to clamber painfully into his chariot and be carried back to the ships.

Odysseus was now the only Greek leader left fighting in the centre, with the Trojans thrusting in upon him from all sides. Grimly he stood his ground and flung them off as a boar at bay flings off the hounds, until an enemy spear pierced his breastplate and left a red wake along his ribs. Odysseus turned on the spearman and, as he fled, drove his own spear between the man's shoulders, letting out the life. Then he pulled out and flung aside the spear that still hung in his own flank and, gathering his breath, shouted three times to his fellow Greeks for aid.

Ajax and Menelaus both heard his shout and came battling through to his side. Menelaus hauled him into his chariot and bore him out of the fighting, while Ajax with his great shield remained behind to hold the centre in Odysseus' place.

Then came Hector thundering back from the left, and the battle roared up around him. Paris loosed another arrow, which sorely wounded Machaon, so that he, whose skill was in tending other men's wounds, must be loaded into a chariot and carried back with a wound in his own hide, to old Nestor's hall for tending.

Now, nearly all the Greek leaders who yet lived were wounded and out of the fight. And the spearmen were again falling back.

All this while Achilles had been standing in the high stern of his ship, watching how the fighting went, and making no move of his own. But when he saw Machaon carried past, dead or sore wounded in the chariot of Nestor, he called to his friend Patroclus and bade him go and find out how it was with him. "For if Machaon be lost to us, it will go ill with the wounded."

Patroclus went swiftly, and found the healer in the hall of Nestor. Hecamede, one of the old king's captive women, was giving him wine with cheese grated into it to revive him, while another pulled out the arrow and dealt with the wound. Nestor was launched on a long story about his own adventures as a young warrior, while Patroclus, desperate for speed, stood in the doorway and tried not to fidget. But when the story was done, he asked his question and was told by Machaon himself that he would live, but that there would be little service to be got out of him for the next few days.

Patroclus was already turning to go when the old king called after him, words that he was to remember afterward. "Tell to your lord Achilles that if he has still no stomach himself for the fighting, then he should send the Myrmidons out under another captain! You are much his size and, wearing his armour, you could give the Trojans to think that Achilles himself had returned to the fight. Then would they be struck with fear, for none of them dares meet him hand to hand!"

Patroclus set out with all speed to rejoin his lord. But again he was delayed, for on the way he met with Eurypolus, another of the leaders, arrow-wounded in the thigh and stumbling painfully back towards his hut.

"Put your arm across my shoulder," Patroclus said, and helped him back to the hut. And then, because the man was a friend and begged him to stay, he cut the barb out with his own dagger, bathed the wound and bound it with bitter salve to ease the pain.

MEANWHILE, HECTOR was urging on the front-fighters of his war-host to cross the ditch, but the chariot horses checked on the brink of it, whinnying in fear, for it was deep and broad and set with sharpened stakes. And between ditch and wall, where the back-driven Greeks were massing, there would be no space to dismount and fight.

Finally the warriors left the charioteers to wait on the far side of the ditch and, forming themselves into five companies, made the crossing on foot, each behind their leaders: behind Hector and Paris, Helenus and Aeneas, with the allies behind Sarpedon, in close formation, joining their oxhide shields into a solid wall as they made their furious charge. The gateway through which the Greek chariots came and went was still open; an escape-way for fleeing warriors, men standing massed and ready on either side. Great Asios, most headstrong of all the Trojans, set his huge chestnut horses straight at it, thinking to crash through. But two champions, both Lapith spearmen from the far north, had taken their stand in the opening and, covered by their comrades throwing rocks and spears from the ramparts on either side, held the attack at bay while the leaves of the great gate were urged to and made fast.

Further along the wall, before another gate,

Hector's company, who should have been foremost in the attack, were hesitating. An eagle, the bird of Zeus, flying over, had dropped a live snake, red as blood, into their midst; this they took for an evil omen. Some even thought that they should call off the attack for that day. But Hector told them, "One omen is best of all – to fight for your country!" This put new heart in them, so that they raised the war shout and thrust forward again where he led.

Further still along the battle line Sarpedon, with Glaucus his friend and sword-brother, were hurling themselves at the wall like mountain lions, the allies storming at their heels. They made a breach in the stockade, but for a while could not break through the defenders who swarmed against them from the inside. Glaucus took an arrow in the arm, and had to retreat to get the barb cut out. Blood spattered on the gate timbers, and the roar and weapon-clash of battle rolled from end to end of the wall.

Hector's company were tearing at the gate timbers, striving to tear down the wall-parapet. But the Greeks within made another parapet of their own shields, and flung down rocks and spears upon them. Then Hector seized a great stone (two men could not have lifted it, but Zeus made it seem to him no heavier than a baled ram's fleece) and he took his stand with legs spread to grip the ground beneath him, and hurled the rock with all his force at the gate before him. The bars burst wide and the timbers shattered and, shouting to his men to follow, he sprang through. With a roar like a torrent breaking free, his men came pouring through the gate and over the palisades on either side. The Greeks were caught up in the flood of their coming and hurled back among their ships.

Then Zeus, having brought the Trojans into the heart of the Greek camp, left the desperate battle swirling under the very sterns of the black galleys, and turned his thoughts elsewhere. But blue-haired Poseidon, lord of the oceans and the earthquake, was looking that way and saw the desperate state of the Greeks. And he harnessed his wind-swift horses to his chariot, and came driving up from his palace beneath the waves, huge sea monsters sporting about him like dolphins around the bows of a ship, until he brought his team plunging ashore below the Greek camp like white rollers breaking on a beach.

There he left them, and went up unseen among the hard-pressed warriors, putting fresh heart into them and urging them to stand firm. And so, not knowing who was amongst them, they stood and strengthened as the power of the god flowed into them. They flung back the Trojans and closed ranks about their ships.

And in the midst of the reeling mass, Hector and Ajax came together. Ajax caught up one of the great stones that were used as chocks under the keels of the ships, and heaved it high. Then he dashed it down upon Hector, catching him over the shield arm and below the helmet strap, so that he dropped like a bull under the axe of sacrifice, with all his armour clanging upon him.

Instantly his companions sprang close about him and, while some guarded their rear and flanks, others bore him off out of the fighting. And seeing great Hector carried off seemingly dead, the Greeks, with Poseidon still unknown in their midst, set up a roar of triumph louder than a storm at sea and surged forward, hurling the Trojans back to the walls and over them and across the ditch on to the open plain.

It was then that Zeus looked again towards Troy. He saw the Trojans in flight, and he saw Hector vomiting black blood as he lay beside the ford of the river Xanthus where his companions had set him down. And he knew that these things were his brother Poseidon's doing. There was little enough he could do about Poseidon, who was almost his equal in power. But he called for Apollo the Sun Lord, the Far-shooter, sender of fear upon men, and bade him go down to where great Hector lay and breathe fresh life into him, and battle-power such as he had never known before.

Apollo went swooping down with the speed of a hawk out of the eye of the sun. He came to where Hector lay, with his companions dashing cold water over him, and breathed fresh life and the strength of his own godhood into him. And Hector rose and called for his armour and turned back to the battle.

The Greeks saw him coming, like a storm cloud coming up against the wind, and fear of him such as they had never known before came upon them. Nevertheless, Ajax and the other front-fighters formed themselves into a great shield of men, to hold him while their comrades fell back on the ships. But Hector, with the Trojan chariots thundering behind him, crashed through their scarce-formed ranks like a flung spear piercing through a hunting buckler. The battle-front broke and scattered, and men were killing men on the open plain, in the ditch, in the broken gateways.

The Trojans had begun to strip the armour from the slain, but Hector shouted to them, "Go straight for the ships and leave the spoils of war! Any man I find lagging behind, I shall see him killed and his body flung to the dogs!"

And he swung his whip full from the shoulder and lashed his horses on, the chariots behind him raising a noise like Zeus' thunder that shakes the mountains, the warriors hurling their spears like lightning shafts as they came.

They flung the chariots forward into the ditch, the horses not swerving aside this time, even from the sharpened stakes, but pouring over as a great sea wave sweeps over the side of a sinking vessel. And over the bodies that already clogged the far side, they swarmed up and over the turf walls and the stockade, sweeping back the Greeks who sought to stand against them. Then they were among the ships, wielding sword and axe, while the Greeks crowding their galley decks sought to drive them back with the long pikes used in sea fighting.

And all the while, in the foremost and fiercest of the struggle, there was Hector with the power of the god still within him. The battle-frenzy shone red behind his eyes, foam like a ram's fleece gathering at the corners of his mouth, the hero-light blazing like a torch above his head. And always he shouted as he went, his voice reaching from end to end of the battle, "Fire! Bring fire for the black ships!"

Men tore brands from the trampled cooking fires and rushed to follow him, whirling the smoking mares'-tails of flame above their heads. The dead fell thick, and the living, led by Hector, plunged up over the clotted mounds of bodies to come aboard the ships, where on the decks the desperate Greeks still stood to hurl them back.

Still the Trojan tide roared on, past the foremost galleys, while Ajax, shouting to his comrades, "Come on! Come against Hector! This is no dance he makes between our ships!" leapt from deck to deck like a man who drives four horses abreast and leaps from the back of one to the back of another, thrusting all the while with a sea-pike as long as three tall men.

Smoke began to rise, and there was a crackle of

flames from old salty ships' timbers; and all the while, above the tumult, rose Hector's trumpet shout, "Fire! Fire the black ships!"

It was then that Patroclus, coming out from the hut of Eurypolus in the furthest part of the camp and upwind of the fighting, saw, as it seemed, half the fleet in flames and the battle whirlpooling around the ships.

WITH HIS HEART sick and hammering within him, Patroclus ran for the camp of the Myrmidons, which the fighting had not yet reached, and the ship where his lord Achilles waited for him.

"Crying, Patroclus?" said his lord when he reached the prow of the ship. "Like a girl child that runs pulling at her mother's skirts to be picked up? Is your father dead? Or mine? Or do you weep for the Greeks dying beside their ships in payment for their own folly?"

Patroclus said, "It is not for their own folly that they die, but for the ill-doing of one man; and he has already offered you full amends – which you have refused." And as he spoke, old wise Nestor's words returned to him. "If you have some reason unknown to us which forbids your return to the fighting, then lend me your armour and your chariot and horses, and let me lead out the Myrmidons in your stead. The Trojans will think that you yourself come against them, and so lose heart. And two thousand well-rested warriors may yet turn the fortunes of the fight."

Then the grief rose in Achilles that he had sworn not to rejoin the war-host until Hector brought fire and sword to his own ships. But this one thing he could do. "Take then my armour and my horses," he said, "and lead the Myrmidons out in my seeming.

Drive the Trojans back lest they fire all our ships and so destroy our road home behind us. But when you have driven them clear of the ships, do not give chase, but return here to me."

So Patroclus promised, and while Achilles himself summoned his war-bands, he put on the splendid armour which all the Trojans knew and feared from the time before Achilles' quarrel with Agamemnon. Automedon, the prince's charioteer, yoked his two immortal horses Xanthus and Balius who had been fathered by the west wind, and put the mortal horse Pedasus, who was as swift and valiant as they, in the side traces. And the Myrmidons, eager as a pack of wolves for the fighting that had been so long denied them, formed themselves into companies and made ready their spears.

Then Patroclus mounted into the chariot and, in close array, shield touching shield behind him, they charged out against the Trojans. Down they came on the enemy flank, and the Trojans saw the armour and horses of Achilles thundering in the lead, and their hearts lurched and sickened within them.

But Achilles did not see their charge, for he was in his hall. He brought out wine in an ancient gold-worked goblet, and poured it, red as blood, on the dry earth before the threshold, and prayed to the All-father. "Lord Zeus, send glory with him, strengthen the heart within him. And when he has driven the fighting back from the ships, let him return to me unharmed, and his sword-companions with him."

And Zeus heard the prayer, and granted one half of it, and refused the other.

Shouting to the Myrmidons to follow, Patroclus was crashing in among the Trojans round the ships, slaying as he went, hurling back the flame-bearers, thrusting after them as they wavered and gave ground and streamed away. And in a while the ships were clear and the fires quenched, and the Trojans out once more beyond the ditch that was now jagged with broken chariots, their horses flying loose across the plain.

After them the horses of Achilles cleared the ditch, and Patroclus flung them forward to come between the Trojans and the walls of their own city, cutting them off and herding them back toward the ranks of the Greeks, who were hastily making ready to receive them.

Many men he slew, on foot and in chariots; chief among them all was Sarpedon, lord of the Lycians and leader of all the Trojan allies. And in the place where Sarpedon fell, the Trojans under Hector rallied about his body, and the fight swirled to and fro until at last the Greeks gained possession of it and stripped it of its splendid armour, and rejoiced. But Sarpedon was son to Zeus by a mortal mother, and in that same moment his body was gone from under their hands, no man knowing how or where, for at his father's order the twin brothers Sleep and Death came unseen on their great wings and bore him away to his own land for burial among his own people.

Now, with the Trojans clear of the ships, Patroclus should have remembered the orders of his prince and turned back. But Zeus the Cloud-gatherer, angry for the death of his son, had put the battle-rage into him so that he forgot all things else. Shouting to Automedon his charioteer, he raced on, slaying as he went, outstripping the Myrmidons until, alone, he reached the walls of Troy. And in his battle-madness, three times he tried to climb the great stones, and three times was beaten back.

Hector, in his chariot in the Scaean Gateway, bade his charioteer drive straight for Achilles – for the man in Achilles' armour – and Patroclus, standing at the foot of the wall, caught up a great stone and flung it at Hector, but missed him, and slew his charioteer. And three times after that, Patroclus charged into the thick of the Trojan battle-mass, each time killing nine men, and always the Myrmidons charging at his heels. And who shall say how the day might have ended? But when he charged a fourth time, the lord Apollo came up behind him, no man seeing, and struck him between the shoulders, so that his eyes darkened and the great helmet fell from his head and rolled clanging under the hooves of the chariot horses.

And men saw his face, that he was Patroclus and not Achilles; his spear shattered and the great shield dropped from his shoulder to the ground. In the circling fight, a Trojan warrior came from behind and drove a spear into his back. Then as Patroclus, with a red mist darkening before his eyes, shortened his spear in his hand and struggled to come at his attacker, Hector came from in front and speared him in the belly, driving the bronze blade right through his body so that he pitched down, and the red mist turned black and his life tore free and fled away.

But with his last breath he spoke to great Hector standing over him. "Death stands close to you also, here in this same gate, and at the hand of the lord Achilles, whose armour I wear."

And there was a breath of silence all about them, for it was known that dying men see far.

Patroclus was dead, and Hector stripped the armour from his body: the armour that had been Achilles' and was a gift from the gods. And drawing a little aside from the fighting, he put it on in place of his own which he sent back into the city for an offering to Athene. Then he plunged back into the struggle that was raging round the champion's naked body.

All through the hot noontide the struggle for possession of the body went on, the Trojans seeking to carry it away and fling it to the dogs in the city, the Greeks to bear it back to the ships for honourable burial.

Automedon, who had served Patroclus as

charioteer, could not join his comrades in the fight at first, for the two chariot horses of Achilles (Pedasus the mortal trace-horse was dead by this time) stood with bowed heads and wept for their lord's friend who had been dear to them through the long years of the siege. They would not move from the spot, either to draw clear of the fighting or to join in. But Zeus saw their grief and, for the sake of their father the west wind, put fire back into their hearts and power into their legs and their arched necks; and then Automedon found himself another warrior to be his charioteer and, with him, plunged back into the struggle.

But little by little, as the sun passed overhead and arched down the sky, the battle began to go against the Greeks. They began to give ground, the Trojans thrusting after. Yet the Myrmidons did not abandon the slain body of Patroclus, but bore it with them, battered and torn like an old cloak, clotted with blood and battle dust, back toward the ships, while Ajax and his companions covered their retreat with broad shields and darting spears.

EVERYWHERE THE WAR-HOST was falling back as Antilochus, the son of Nestor, went speeding to tell Achilles of his friend's death, in the hope that the black news would at last bring him again into the fighting.

He came panting to Achilles in his hall, where he had been pacing to and fro, hearing the sounds of battle and sick to know how the fighting went, and gasped out his evil tidings. "Patroclus is dead, and they are fighting for his naked body, for Hector has his armour!"

Achilles spoke no word, but flung himself face down beside the hearth-fire, and threw ashes and black dust over the brightness of his hair until Antilochus grasped his hands, fearing that he would slay himself in the wildness of his grief.

Then came Thetis his mother, up from the sea-depths to comfort him. But he swore that he would not live, except to slay Hector who had slain his friend.

"You cannot go into battle without armour," said his mother, her white arms about him. "You will not live long enough to come at Hector through the spears. Let you wait through this one night, and I will go to Hephaestus, lord of all armourers, and in the morning I will bring you such a shield and helmet and breastplate as has not been seen by mortal men."

And so saying, she was gone, and her voice no more than the tide sighing along the shore.

Meanwhile, the struggle for Patroclus' hacked and battered body had reached almost to the ship-wall.

With the grief tearing at him like a wild beast Achilles went out, unarmoured as he was, and climbed up to the highest rampart and took his stand there against the red flare of the sunset. Fire seemed to spring up from the crown of his head, like the beacon-blaze that summons help for a town attacked at night. And there he stood and shouted aloud in defiance of the Trojans, clear as men raise the battle cry when they race to the attack on a city wall.

Three times he shouted, and three times the Trojan horses neighed in fear and swerved back from the ditch, and three times the men of Troy felt their hearts shaken with terror. And they lost purpose and fell apart, so that the Myrmidons drew the body of Patroclus clear of the battle-dust and bore it in through the gate in the ship-wall.

The gates were forced shut and guarded. They laid Patroclus on a bier and Achilles came beside him, weeping that he had sent his sword-brother with chariot and horses into battle in his stead, and would never see him come driving back.

They bore the torn body to Achilles' hall, and the slave women, weeping also, for he had been kind even to them, bathed away the blood and filth of the battlefield and lapped him in white cloth, with all gentleness.

And the sun set, and the quiet night came down.

Some of Hector's leaders would have had him withdraw for safety within the walls of Troy, for it was sure that next morning Achilles would be among the front-fighters once again, and then they would be in deadly peril. But Hector said, "Have you not had your fill of city walls? Let Achilles come. We shall meet him on the open plain."

And so again the plain was star-speckled among the tamarisk bushes and the ancient grave-mounds with the camp-fires of the Trojans and their allies.

And before the hall of Achilles the women keened for Patroclus, and the Myrmidons mourned for him, Achilles above all, with his head upon the still breast of his friend.

And in his great house on Olympus, with Thetis looking on, Hephaestus set his forge-fires roaring with the breath of twenty oxhide bellows. He took bronze and silver, tin and gold, and made a splendid breastplate and shin-guards, a tall crested helm of the reddest gold, and a great shield on which were inlaid in precious metals pictures of cities and seas and battles, a lion hunt, fields where the corn was being harvested, vineyards heavy with grapes, and men and women dancing to the voice of flutes.

In the dawn, Thetis of the Silver Feet came down

from high Olympus bearing the armour which Hephaestus had made for her son. And Achilles put on the gleaming gear, and with it such a heart for war and vengeance as even he had never known before. But Odysseus, who knew the rules of honour and how such things should be done, would not let him take the Myrmidons into battle until the peace had been properly made between him and Agamemnon, with a sacrifice to the gods and all due ceremonies, and until Agamemnon had made over all the gifts which Achilles had refused before.

Agamemnon sent for the gifts, and when they were brought, stood up and spoke his sorrow for the wrong that he had done. And Achilles, who did not now want them, the gold and the slaves and the fine horses, even the girl Briseis, accepted them because that was the quickest way to be done with them and get on to the fighting. So at last peace was made between them.

Then the Myrmidons and all the war-host ate their morning meal. But Achilles would not touch food or wine until Patroclus should be avenged.

He mounted into his chariot, and would have been off and away. But Xanthus, who was given the power of human speech for that one time by the goddess Hera, bowed his head until his long mane brushed the ground and said, "Lord Achilles, the sorrow is upon us that though we bear you swiftly as our father the west wind, yet our speed will not save you, for your death-time is near at hand."

"That I know well," said Achilles. "But I will not turn from the fight while Hector lives, so give me your speed meanwhile."

And they shook their manes and sprang towards the enemy.

All that day, at the head of his Myrmidons, Achilles harried and slew the Trojans. He forced them into the river; and though the river, defending its own people, came down upon him in a spate the colour of blood, and all but washed him away, he crossed after them and slew them on the far side. Slew and slew until the earth ran crimson and the horses, trampling on dead men, flung up great gouts of blood to spatter the axle and rails of the chariot. So he pressed on, wild to win glory; he and the war-host and the fire together drove the Trojans back to the walls of their city, and sent them streaming in through the city gates that had been dragged wide to receive them.

But Hector stood alone before the Scaean Gate, his spear in his hand. And from the gatehouse roof the king his father, seeing him there, and Achilles in his god-given armour rushing toward him like a shooting star, called down to him in an agony to come within the gate. But Hector stood unmoving and waited for Achilles, as though for a meeting agreed between them long since.

He stayed because his doom was upon him and

held him there. And he stayed because he knew that, by keeping the war-host out on the plain the night before, he had brought this death and destruction upon his own men, and unless he could avenge them by slaying Achilles, he must pay the debt with his own life.

But as Achilles sprang from his chariot and rushed towards him, Hector's courage snapped, as it had never done before in all the years since the black ships came. He sprang back, and turned and ran. Three times round the walls of Troy; three times past the sacred fig tree and the well where the women used to wash their clothes in time of peace, Hector running like a stag and Achilles leaping leopard-like on his heels. Then, as it had gone, so Hector's courage returned to him, and when they came for the third time to the Scaean Gate, he turned to face his enemy.

Achilles' flung spear whistled over his shoulder, so close that he felt the wind of it. He flung his own spear in return, but the point could not pierce the wonderful shield with its cities and wars and flute dancers.

Achilles had one spear left, but now Hector had none. He ripped his sword from its sheath, and crying, "Let me not die without honour!" sprang at Achilles.

But before he came within sword-strike, Achilles drove the remaining spear straight through his neck, bringing him stumbling and choking to the ground. "Dogs and ravens shall tear your flesh unburied!" said Achilles, looking down at him in the dust.

Hector made one plea. "Take the gold that my father will pay, and give him back my body to be buried with honour —"

But Achilles was beyond even that mercy. "Hound! I would tear and eat your flesh myself, if I could bear to do it! But the dogs shall have it to fight over, though your father offers me your weight in gold!"

Then Hector pleaded no more, but with his last breath strangling in his throat he said, "Then when Paris my brother shall slay you in this same gate, remember me." And the last breath went from him and his eyes darkened, and his soul took its way to the land of the dead.

And while Achilles stripped from him the armour that a day since had been his own, men came from among the Greek front-fighters to look on his beauty now that they need no longer fear him, and each man shortened his spear and added his own stab-wound to Hector's body before he drew back.

Then Achilles did a hideous thing. He cut through Hector's ankles behind the tendons that run from heel to calf, and threaded through broad thongs of oxhide and made them fast to the framework of his chariot. Then he loaded the recaptured armour into the chariot also and, mounting into it himself, he seized the reins and whipped up the horses so that they sprang away swift as the west wind back toward the ships.

And as they went, Hector's body was dragged

behind them, twisting and lurching over the rough ground, his dark hair flying and fouled with dust and all the filth of the battlefield.

HECTOR'S MOTHER and all her women, crowding the battlements above the Scaean Gate, raised a piteous shriek and began to wail and lament for Hector slain. Andromache was in the high chamber of their house, weaving a mantle of fine purple bordered with golden flowers, while the bower-maidens heated water for her lord to wash when he came home from the fighting. She heard the wailing from the walls, and the shuttle fell from her hand. She cried out that she heard the voice of her husband's mother, and called two of her maidens to come with her, and ran from the house to see why the people lamented.

She reached the gate-tower, and from its high viewpoint saw Hector's body in a cloud of dust, being dragged behind Achilles' chariot toward the ships. And she dropped like a wounded bird among all the wailing women. Then, coming to herself again, she took up the lament, wailing for her babe left without a father, and for Hector who was worse than slain, for lacking proper burial rites he would not pass free to the realms of Hades, but must wander lonely and uncomforted in the borderlands between the living and the dead.

But Hector was not the only one of the heroes to lie unburied that night.

While Achilles slept the sleep of a lion glutted with much killing, the ghost of Patroclus came and stood beside him and said, "Why do you not yet burn and bury me? For the other shades of dead men will not let me join their company, and lonely I wander outside the dark gates of Hades. Yet take my hand once more, for when I have gone at last beyond those gates, there can be no more coming back for me."

And Achilles tried to put his arms around his sword-brother, but he could feel nothing, and the vision wisped away like smoke. Then he awoke; and at once he sent men to cut down trees for a funeral pyre.

From as far inland as the forests of Mount Ida they brought wood, loaded on mules, to the shore. And there, in the place that Achilles bade them, they built a great pyre; and on it they laid the body of Patroclus; and each of his companions cut mourning locks of their hair to scatter over him.

The thick mane of his own hair Achilles hacked off and set in his dead friend's hands. Many cattle he slew in his friend's honour, and laid them on the pyre together with four chariot horses and two of his favourite hounds. Lastly, being mad with grief and rage, he slit the throats of twelve Trojan captives and laid them on the pyre. They stacked jars of oil and honey around the sides. Then at sunset Achilles thrust torches into the pile; and the wood caught, and the fat and honey. The north wind and the west wind came and blew upon the flames, and the pyre blazed all night long, until in the grey light of morning the flames died down.

Then they put the ashes of Patroclus into a great golden cup, a two-handled cup from which he and Achilles had often drunk together. And they set it on the ground and built over it a rough chamber of stone, and over that they raised a tall mound of earth. But they did not seal the stone chamber, for Achilles gave orders that when he also was dead, they should mingle his ashes with the ashes of his friend in the same cup.

And then it was time for the funeral games which must be held in the dead man's honour, according to the custom.

The prizes were brought out from Achilles' own treasure store; and all day the games went on. First came the chariot race. Five champions took part, the best chariots and the best horses and the best drivers in all the war-host. They whirled away over the plain, the dust-clouds rising behind them, round the ancient mark-stone that served as a turning point and back again to the men watching for them beside the ships.

Diomedes came in first, whipping his horses on, shouting and singing to them, the wheels of his chariot scarce touching the ground to leave a track in the dust. To him went the first prize: a woman slave skilled in music and the household arts, and a three-footed cauldron all of gold.

Next came in Antilochus, Nestor's son, who had overtaken Menelaus by his driving skill more than the speed of his horses, and Menelaus so close behind that the thunder of their hooves came as one. To them went the second and third prizes, a fine mare and a lesser cauldron, to be shared between them as they pleased. Then came Meriones, and a long way after, Eumelus, who had met with trouble, dragging his broken chariot himself and driving the horses ahead of him. But for them also there were lesser prizes from the treasure of Achilles.

Then came the boxing match. Up stood Epeius, a giant among men and a famous boxer, and Euryalus, a leader among the men of Argos, to fight it out, each stripped to a loincloth and belted with broad leather thongs. They put up their fists to each other, and the battle was long and hard, the sweat rolling off their bodies. At last Epeius laid Euryalus out with a blow to the cheekbone, and so received the working mule, which was the prize, while the other sat on the ground dazed and spitting blood.

After that came the wrestling. Ajax and Odysseus (his wound scarcely healed) struggled together like a pair of antlered stags in the mating season. But they were so well matched that neither could gain a clear victory, and in the end Achilles bade them break off and share the prize between them.

But in the foot race which followed after, Odysseus

was the clear winner, and the prize a silver bowl for mixing wine.

Last of all, Achilles caused the armour of Sarpedon to be brought and set up on a spear in the midst of the gathering, and called for two champions to fight with spears; the armour to go to the man who drew first blood. Diomedes and great Ajax put on their armour and came together in the clear space at the centre of the gathering.

Three times they hurled together and three times they fought close. Their blood growing hot, Ajax struck through the light shield of Diomedes but did not pierce his breastplate, and Diomedes aimed a blow at Ajax's thick neck over the rim of his shield. All the onlookers shouted to them to stop, fearing the death of one or the other. And so the fight ended without the shedding of blood, and the two champions shared the armour of Sarpedon. And the sun being near to setting, they went to feast in Achilles' hall.

But when the feasting was over and all men had gone to their own sleeping places, there was no sleep for Achilles; and in the darkness he wept for Patroclus and the loss of all that they had known and shared together. At last he sprang up and went down to the seashore and fell to pacing the desolate tide-line until the darkness paled into the dawn. But there was no comfort for him in the new morning; and, like a man driven out of his wits by grief, he went up to the horse-yard and yoked up his horses and led them to where the body of Hector still lay face down in the dust. He bound him again to the chariot-tail, and so drove out of the camp and three times round dead Patroclus' grave-mound, dragging dead Hector behind him in the dust.

Again and again, for twelve nights and twelve days, he did the same. But during all that time Apollo wrapped the body in his protection so that it took no further harm from the savage treatment. And at the end of that time, the gods in anger agreed that the great Achilles was dishonouring himself, his friend and the earth itself in his madness, and the thing must cease.

THE GODS sent for the lady Thetis, and bade her go tell her son that Zeus and all the gods of Olympus grew angry with him for his treatment of Hector's body, and that he must give it back to Priam his father, for the honourable ransom which the old king would pay.

And Achilles listened to his mother when she came beside him, her words reaching him through his grief as no one else's could have done.

At the same time the gods sent Iris, the Lady of the Rainbow, who often acted as their messenger, to Priam where he sat grieving in his palace with the dust and ashes of mourning on his head. They bade her tell him that now he should go to Achilles and offer the proper ransom for his son's body, telling him also that if he did so, Achilles would listen to him.

The old king went to his treasury and opened his chests of carved and scented wood, and brought out twelve fine robes and twelve white mantles and richly embroidered tunics. Ten bars of yellow gold he added to the pile, and gleaming cauldrons, and a beautiful golden cup, the pride of his heart, which had been given to him by the people of Thrace. Then he called for his remaining sons, Paris and Deiphobus and the rest, and, railing at them in his grief for being still alive when Hector was dead, he bade them make ready a waggon and load the ransom into it.

And when they had yoked the mules and loaded in the treasure as he bade them, he prayed and poured wine to the gods, and mounted into his chariot which had also been made ready for him. Alone, save for the drivers and a herald, he drove out through the Scaean Gate and away over the plain in the darkness, toward the ships.

But unknown to him, the god Hermes, Lord of Wayfaring, went with him, and with his winged rod cast sleep into the eyes of all who looked that way, so that no man saw them pass, the old king in his chariot and the piled treasure-waggon. So they passed unchallenged through the camp until they reached the reed-thatched hall of Achilles. Priam got down from the chariot and went in, while Achilles' men set about unloading the waggon, and the god was on his own way back to Olympus.

Achilles was in his hall, surrounded by his companions with the remains of supper in their midst. The old king went in and knelt down at the prince's feet, and took and kissed his hands according to the custom. Hands that seemed to him crimson and terrible with the death of so many of his sons beside the beloved Hector.

"Have pity on me and listen to the word of the gods and give me back my dead son," he begged. "Think of your own father, who is old and grieving, even as I;

though for him there is still hope of his living son's return. Have pity on me; for my son's sake I have done what I did not think possible and kissed the hands that slew him and his brothers."

And Achilles thought of his own father, far away, who was indeed old, and who he knew would soon have as good cause as Priam for his grieving. He raised the old king from his knees and spoke kindly to him, and they wept, both of them together; Priam for his son, and Achilles for his father and for Patroclus his friend.

Then Achilles bade the women make Hector's body ready for burial and cover him with a white mantle, the finest that his father had brought in the treasure-waggon. And when that was done, and Hector's body laid in the now empty waggon, he sent for more food and wine, and he and the old king ate and drank together, before Priam set out with the ransomed body of his son, back across the dark plain to the waiting city of Troy.

All the people of the city came to meet them in the gate, lamenting and crying out for Hector. They carried his body into his own house and laid it on the bed in the high chamber. The women gathered round, keening for him, singing the death songs, tearing their bright hair.

Andromache led the lament, sitting at the head of the bed and holding his head between her hands.

"My husband, you are gone from life too young, leaving me a widow in your house, and your son without a father. You did not die in your bed, holding out your hands to me, or speaking me some last word that I could remember through all the nights and days of the long years that I must weep for you."

Then Hecuba his mother took up the lament. "Hector, dearest to me by far of all my sons; when you were alive you were beloved of the gods, and surely they love you still, for they have allowed no mark nor blemish to show how you were dragged behind your slayer's chariot wheels. Save for the one red flower of your death-wound, you lie as though you slept."

Then rose Helen, the third to lead their lamentations, dark-robed and with white arms unflung. "Hector, nearest to my heart of all the brothers of my husband's house, in all the years since he brought me here — would that I had died before those years began — never did I hear a word from you that was bitter or ungentle, and when others upbraided me for my ill-doing, you would restrain them with your kind heart and gentle words. Oh woe to me, woe to me, for there is no one now in all Troy to stand my friend."

Then Priam the king bade the people yoke up the oxen and fetch wood for a funeral pyre, telling them that they need fear no Greek attack while they did so, for Achilles had granted eleven days' truce while they buried Hector. So they went out with their ox-carts, and for nine days they brought in wood and built a great pyre outside the city walls, and on the tenth day they laid Hector's body on the crest of it, and plunged torches deep into its heart.

And when the fire sank, they took the ashes and charred bones and wrapped them in fine purple cloth, weeping all the while. They put them in a golden box and laid the box in a chamber hollowed in the earth, and covered it with stones and piled a grave-mound over it in haste, keeping look-outs on all sides, for the eleven days of peace were almost up.

Then they went back into the city and held a great feast according to their proper custom.

Such was the burial that they gave to Hector, Tamer of Horses.

THE LUCK OF TROY

AFTER THE TRUCE-DAYS for Hector's burial the siege wore slowly on, just as it had done for close on ten years already. Even Achilles seemed to have lost his thirst for battle, while the Trojans, now that their war-leader was dead, no longer dared to thrust out beyond their walls into the open plain.

Also, the Trojans were waiting for new allies to come to their aid: fighting men from the south, led by their king Memnon, the Son of the Bright Dawn; and a strong war-band of women warriors, the Amazons. And so, waiting, they remained quiet within their city gates.

Now everyone knew, Greeks as well as Trojans, that in the temple of Athene in the high citadel of Troy was a sacred image, a black stone shaped like Athene's shield, which had fallen from heaven long ago. The Palladium, men called it; but they also called it the Luck of Troy, and believed that while it was there the grey-eyed goddess would help them to keep all enemies out of the city. So they guarded it day and night, and took strength and comfort from knowing that it was there.

It had long seemed to Odysseus that it would be a fine thing to steal the Luck of Troy from its guarded temple in the midst of the city. Surely the Trojans would take its loss as a terrible omen and lose whatever heart was still in them. He began to think how the thing might be done; and soon he had worked out a plan.

There was a king of the island of Delos who had three daughters. It was said that one of them could turn water into wine, and one could turn stones into bread, and the youngest could turn mud into olive oil. The Greeks were weary of paying gold to the Phoenician traders for their supplies of corn and wine and oil. So Odysseus went to the High King and asked leave to take one of his ships to Delos to fetch the three princesses, if they would come. As there was no fighting going on, Agamemnon agreed, and he went aboard his ship with fifty of his own men at the oars, and sailed away, promising to return within the month.

Next day an aged beggar appeared in the Greek camp, leaning on a staff and clad in filthy rags with a half-bald stag-skin by way of a cloak. He came crouching and grinning to the hut of Diomedes, and squatted in the doorway. Diomedes tossed him a handful of bread and meat and after he had eaten, gnawing the bone like a dog, asked him who he was and where he came from.

The beggar told a long story of how he had been a Cretan pirate captured by Egyptians, and how he had worked many years in their stone quarries, until he had escaped by hiding among the great stones carried down the Nile by raft for building a temple on the seashore, and got aboard a Phoenician trading ship. How the ship had been wrecked on the coast away south of Troy, and he alone had survived, being washed ashore clinging to a piece of broken planking.

It was a good story, and when it was told, Diomedes gave him a rug and let him sleep in the fore-porch of the hut.

Next day the old wretch went round the camp, begging and talking with the warriors. And from then on it seemed that they could never be rid of him. Wherever he was, he stirred up quarrels, and if there was an ugly story about any of the chiefs or their fathers or grandfathers, he knew it and told it to all around. So he got a buffet from Agamemnon's staff, and Ajax kicked him, and Idomeneus thumped him with a spear butt for a tale about his grandmother.

At last he stole a gold cup from Nestor – the beautiful two-handed cup with a dove on each handle – and when it was found in his dirty pouch everyone cried out that that was enough and he must be whipped out of the camp.

Some of the young warriors, laughing and shouting, dragged him off across the plain and right up to the gates of Troy. And holding him there, the leader of the band, Nestor's son Thrasymedes, called out to those within, "We are sick of this shameless beggar, so we are going to whip him well, and then you may have him if you want him, or he may wander until he starves, but if he comes back to us, we shall put out his eyes and cut off his hands and feet and give what's left to the camp dogs."

The young men of Troy laughed also when they heard this, and gathered on the walls to watch. They whipped him with their bowstrings until the blood ran from his shoulders and he ceased from howling and lay as though dead. Then they left him with a parting kick, and went their way.

The beggar lay still for a while, then sat up, wiping his eyes and shouting curses after them. Then he tried to stand up, but his legs gave under him, and he crawled on hands and knees into the gateway, and sat there crying and groaning with the end of the stag-skin pulled over his head.

Helen, who was on the gatehouse roof and had seen all that passed, was sorry for him, and she came down the stair and bade the men on guard to open up a leaf of the gate as they did when there were supplies to be brought in. When they had done so, she went out with her pretty skirts gathered close, and spoke to the poor wretch kindly, asking him why he had been used so cruelly.

He groaned and rubbed his shoulders, and in a while answered her that he was a poor man who had been shipwrecked and was trying to beg his way home, but that the Greeks suspected him of being a Trojan spy. Then, peering up at her through tangled hair, he said that if she were Helen of the Fair Cheeks, as her beauty told him she must be, then he had been in her own country not long ago and could tell her of her father and her brothers (who were long since dead, though she did not know it) and the little daughter she had left behind her.

Then Helen wept, for it was many years since she had had word of her kin.

She raised the beggar who was crouching at her feet, and bade him follow her. And she turned back into the city, walking with her bower-maidens at either hand and the beggar hobbling after, until she came to her own house within the palace courts of the old king.

Paris was not there, and she ordered the bath to be filled with warm water, and fresh clothes to be brought. She set herself to washing his hurts and anointing him with the finest oil, for there was a suspicion growing in her mind about this beggar. All the while that she was washing and anointing him, while the dirt fell away, the suspicion grew; and when she had combed his thick hair and clothed him in a white tunic and a mantle of the deepest purple, and she saw him in his proper seeming, she knew him for Odysseus, who had been her friend in the days of her youth.

Almost, she cried out, but he laid a finger on his lips, and bade her, "Hush!" And she remembered the greatness of his danger, here in the midst of his enemies.

"You are the strange one!" she said, shivering

and weeping. "How have you borne to be thus beaten and disgraced, all to come within the walls of Troy?"

"I have good reason," Odysseus told her, but glanced toward the door, wondering whether Paris might come through it at any moment and discover them.

She saw the look and understood it, and said without thought, "Paris my lord is far from home, gone to meet Penthesilea and her Amazons, who are coming to bring their aid to Troy."

Odysseus smiled an inward-turning smile, and she saw that also, and knew what she had said, and wept again. "Grief upon me! Now I have betrayed to you the last hope of my marriage-people. And if you escape out of Troy you must tell it to your own kind, and they will take the Amazons by ambush and slay them all! If it were not for the old friendship between us, I would call to the guards that you are here, and they would give your body to the dogs and fix your head above the Scaean Gate!"

"Lady," Odysseus told her, "we two are indeed friends from of old, and your friend I shall remain when the Greeks break into Troy at last, to slay the men and carry off the women. In that time, if I yet live, no harm shall come to you; but safely and honourably you shall return to the house of King Menelaus. And I swear to you by all the gods that I will tell to no other man the thing that you have just told to me."

Then Helen set before him meat and wine, but after he had eaten and drunk and something of his strength had come back to him, he said, "Now I must put on my dirt and rags again, and take up my pouch and my staff to beg my way through the city."

When he stood ready to leave, Helen bethought herself that she would make him a parting gift for old friendship's sake. She went to a painted olive-wood chest against the wall, and brought out a delicate phial of gold, wrought into the shapes of beasts and flowers.

"Always, in these times, I am wretched save when sleep comes to me," she said. "Therefore I have come to look upon sleep as the best of all gifts. A queen of Egypt gave me this, on our way to Troy. It is a drug that brings quiet sleep even to the most unhappy, pressed from the poppy pods which garland the head of the god of sleep. This one phial I give to you, that even in Troy you may not go from Helen without a gift in remembrance. Even if you do not need the sleep, the flask has its value and its beauty."

And she gave it to Odysseus, who placed it carefully in his pouch, together with the fine clothes that she had given him. A sword also she gave him, which he stowed under his rags.

"If you see me in the street, take no heed of me," he said. "I shall salute you only as a beggar who has been kindly treated in your house. Only keep your heart up, lady, for the end of your sorrow draws near."

And he went out from the house and the palace courtyards into the streets of Troy.

For a while he remained in the city, giving people time to be used to the sight of him. By day he begged through the streets, and at night he sought shelter in one or other of the temples. No one thought this odd, for it was the custom for folk who were sick or in trouble, to sleep at night on the floor of a temple, hoping that the god would send a dream to tell them how their sickness might be healed or their sorrow eased.

On the last night he slept in the temple of Athene, where the black stone that was the Luck of Troy lay always on the altar, and where the priestesses kept watch in turn, all through the night, with temple guards always within call. That night Odysseus lay on the temple floor among all the other people seeking dreams from the goddess. But he sought no dream, and lay wakeful all night long until the last priestess came to take the final watch.

She walked up and down barefoot among the sleeping people, a torch in her hand, murmuring prayers to grey-eyed Athene. She passed Odysseus and went on; and while her back was towards him he took the golden phial from his pouch and laid it beside him on the marble pavement. By the time she turned back in her pacing, he lay still again with eyes closed as though deep in sleep.

When the priestess came past again, the light from her torch fluttered on the small beautiful thing lying there, and she stooped and picked it up and looked at it curiously. The stopper seemed a little loose, and a fragrance stole from it that was like the scent of all the flowers in the country of her youth.

She opened it and sniffed, then tongue-tip tasted the syrupy drug. It seemed to her the sweetest taste that ever she had known, and she tasted again and again, more and more deeply, until she found the flask was nearly empty. Then, guiltily, she pushed in the stopper and laid the flask down again, and moved on, murmuring her prayer.

But soon a great drowsiness came over her and she sank down before the altar and fell asleep, deeply and more deeply asleep. The torch in her hand drooped toward the pavement and guttered out, and the temple was dark.

Then Odysseus put the flask back in his pouch and, getting up, crept between the sleeping figures to the altar and, feeling in the dark, took up from it the stone shape that was the Luck of Troy. He stowed it in his pouch under the broken food that he had saved from that day's begging, replacing it with a copy that he had made beforehand of blackened clay. Then he returned to his place among the sleepers and lay down again until the light of dawn stole between the sanctuary columns. The sleepers woke and the temple gates were opened, and he walked out with the rest.

Outside, few people were yet astir in the streets, but he kept to the shadows, all the same, and leaned heavily on his staff, dragging himself along until he came to the eastern gate which faced toward the hills and away from the Greek camp. He told the warriors on guard there that he had collected enough food to get him to another town, and was minded to be on his way. He opened his pouch to show them the mess of broken bread and meat that hid the other things beneath. And the warriors laughed and wished him a town with richer pickings than Troy, and passed him through.

He hobbled off along the waggon road that led toward the forests of Mount Ida. And when he reached the fringes of the trees and knew that he was out of sight from the city, he turned aside from the track and lay down under their deep-layered shade. And there he slept until the light began to fade and the evening coolness woke him.

Then he got up and emptied out his pouch. He ate the food of yesterday's begging (he was hungry, and it would be a while yet before he reached the Greek camp). He washed himself in the chill waters of a mountain stream, and put on the clothes which Helen had given him, slung the sword-belt over his shoulder and stowed the Palladium in the breast of his tunic. Then he set out once more, following the stream between high wooded banks until at last it reached the river Xanthus.

Soon he came to an outpost guarding the far end of the Greek camp. And when the warriors saw Odysseus in the light of their watch-fire they cried out in surprise and greeting, for his ship had not yet returned from Delos.

Odysseus told them some story of getting sea-weary and bidding his men put him ashore to stretch his legs by a walk back to camp while they saw to some needful repairs to the ship. Then he bade the men of the outpost a quiet night and walked on, into the camp, to the hall of Agamemnon, where the High King and the chiefs and captains were feasting.

They, too, leapt up in surprise at his coming, and Agamemnon demanded if he had brought the princesses who could make corn and wine and oil.

"No," said Odysseus, "but I have brought something else that I think may be of even greater use to us." And from under his mantle he brought out the Luck of Troy, holding it up for all to see. To Nestor's son he added, "And when next you drive out a beggar, do not you beat him so hard or so long!" And he hitched at his shoulders as he spoke.

Then there was a gale of laughter and much rejoicing among the Greeks, who were once again full of hope, now that the Luck was in their hands. And they sacrificed ten oxen to Zeus.

But within the walls of Troy there was shock and despair at the loss of their sacred treasure, and many of the Trojans felt that their last hope was gone.

MEANWHILE, PARIS was guiding the Amazons into Troy. The Amazons were a tribe of women warriors who lived far away in the lands watered by the river Thermodon. In battle they were the equals of the strongest men, and some said that they were daughters of Ares, the god of war.

Penthesilea, their young queen, had accidentally slain her sister Hippolyta out hunting when a spear she had thrown at a deer struck her instead. And in her bitter sorrow, for she loved her sister deeply, Penthesilea could find no sweetness left in life, and had no wish but to die also. But it must be gloriously and in battle. So she and the maidens of her bodyguard had left the forests and wide streams of their own country and come riding to join the defenders of Troy.

Led by Paris, who knew better than anyone else the forest tracks and the high hill passes, they reached the city without a blow struck on the way. Odysseus had kept his promise of silence to Helen of the Fair Cheeks, and so there was no band of Greeks waiting in ambush for their coming.

The people of Troy came swarming to greet them when they rode in, astonished to see them riding on horseback, which was the custom of their country, instead of driving in chariots in the usual way.

They thronged about Penthesilea, who shone among her maidens like the moon among stars, tossing up spears in greeting, throwing flowers beneath her horse's hooves, kissing her feet.

Priam held a great feast for her coming, and gave her golden cups and fine embroidered garments and a sword with a silver hilt. And she held up the sword and swore that with it she would slay Achilles. But when Andromache heard of the vow she said within herself, "Unhappy girl! If Hector could not do that thing, what chance have you? And the piled earth lies over Hector."

Next morning, Penthesilea rose from sleep and put on her bright armour, her new sword at her side. She took her spears and her strong shield, and mounted her white warhorse, and with her twelve maidens beside her, and Hector's brothers and kindred, she set herself at the head of the Trojan war-host and rode out wind-swift toward the Greek camp and the black ships on the distant shoreline.

And the Greeks, seeing her come as they drew up their own battle lines, asked each other, "Who is this that leads the Trojans as Hector used to lead them? Surely it is some god who rides at the head of the charioteers!"

So the plain of Troy ran red as though with poppies, as it had done so many times before, and the warrior maidens took a heavy toll of the best and bravest of the Greeks. But before the sun was past its height half of them lay slain; and then grief and rage came upon their queen. She hurled herself upon the chariots, mad to avenge her bodyguard, driving the warriors as a lioness drives cattle among the hills, and shouting as she rode, "This is the day you pay for the sorrows of Priam! Diomedes! Achilles! Ajax! You who men say are the bravest of your breed, come out now to meet my spears!"

Again and again she charged at the head of Priam's household, the few who remained of her bodyguard still about her, and the chariots that followed her lurching and rocking over the bodies of the slain. Like a lightning flash among storm clouds she went, now here, now there, and the Greeks were yet again hurled back across their ditch, and men were among them with firebrands to burn the black ships as on the day of the battle-rage of Hector.

Achilles and Ajax had not heard the start of the fighting, for they had been away from the camp on a raid of their own, but, returning just as Penthesilea and the Trojans crossed the ditch, they flung themselves into the struggle to drive them back from the ships. Ajax paid no heed to the Amazons but rushed upon the men of Troy, while Achilles charged against Penthesilea and slew the last five maidens of her bodyguard. And she, seeing her dearest maidens dead, rode straight for the two Greek champions.

She flung her spear at Achilles, but it fell back

blunted from his great shield. She flung a second at Ajax, crying, "I am the daughter of the god of war, feel now my spear!" But his armour also withstood her spear point, and he and Achilles laughed out loud.

And laughing still, Achilles raised the great spear that none but he could handle, and even as her hand flew to her sword-hilt, he drove it down through the worked bronze and deep into her breast so that the red blood fountained as he dragged out the blade. Then, with shortened spear, he stabbed her white horse, so that both came down together, dying in the same fall.

Penthesilea lay in the churned dust, like a young poplar tree that the wind has overthrown. Her helmet had fallen off, and the Greeks who gathered round marvelled to see her so young and so fair to look upon, with her bright hair spilled about her. And the heart of Achilles who had killed her was pierced with grief and pity, and he wept over her, now that she was dead.

The Greeks, in pity also, did not go after the Trojans, who were again falling back, nor did they strip the armour from the queen and her spear-maidens, but laid them each on a bier and sent them back in peace to Priam.

And Priam, who last night had made a feast for them, had their bodies burned on a tall pyre and their ashes put into golden caskets, and buried them in the grave-mound of one of Troy's long-dead kings.

THE CHIEFS AND PRINCES and old men of Troy gathered in council. With the king, they decided that they should withdraw within the walls until King Memnon, who could not be far behind the Amazons, should reach them with the great band of Ethiopians that he was bringing to their aid. Polydamas, the most cool-headed of them all, argued that there should be no more waiting and no more war, but the Trojans should return Helen to her own people, with twice the jewels that she had brought with her from the house of Menelaus. At that, Paris sprang up in rage, calling Polydamas a coward; for the fate of Troy mattered little to him if he might keep Helen to himself for a while longer yet.

And the Trojan war-host withdrew again, and waited within its walls. In a while King Memnon came; the most beautiful of all men save for Paris and Achilles, and leading a great war-band of men who had nothing white about them but their teeth, so fiercely had the sun kissed them in the land from which they came.

Then Priam made another feast, and gave to King Memnon a great cup of gold, wine-filled to the brim. And Memnon drank it dry at one draught. But he made no boast of what he would do in battle. "If I am a good fighting man, that will be known when the fighting starts," he said. "Meanwhile, let us sleep, for to bide wakeful and drinking wine all night is a poor way to make ready for battle in the morning."

The morning came, and Memnon led his dark war-host out on to the plain. The hearts of the Greeks would have sunk within them as they saw the bands of fresh and unwearied warriors, had not Achilles in his shining armour given them courage.

Memnon fell upon the left wing of the Greek army, and there he and Nestor's son Antilochus came together. Memnon leapt upon the young prince like a black lion upon a kid, and Antilochus heaved up a carved stone from a nearby tomb of ancient kings, and struck out with it, sending Memnon reeling back from the blow to his helmet. But the dark king came to his feet again on the instant, and drove his spear through Antilochus' breast-armour and deep into his heart, so that he fell dead before the eyes of his old father.

Memnon charged again, slaying right and left, and stripping the armour from the dead. But Nestor, driven back from the body of his son, climbed into his chariot and forced a way through to Achilles, begging him to come with all speed to save Antilochus' body from dishonour.

Achilles sped to the place where the young man had fallen, and so came face to face with King Memnon, who swung his team back to meet him. Memnon heaved a great stone at him, but Achilles fended it on his shield and ran on forward, wounding Memnon in the shoulder; but wounded though he was, the dark king drew back his spear and drove in a thrust that wounded Achilles in the arm.

Little heed Achilles paid to that, though the red blood ran down, for it was not in the arm that he could receive his death-wound. And they drew their swords and flew together, and with sweeping blade-strokes they lashed at each other on shield and helmet. Their long horsehair crests were hacked off and went like ragged birds down a high wind, while their shields rang to the sword-strokes. They thrust at the knee below the shield rim and at the throat between shield and helmet strap. The dust flew up in a cloud from beneath their trampling feet.

At last, Achilles made a thrust so swift that Memnon failed to parry it. The bronze blade drove clean through below the breastbone and he crashed to the ground with the life driven from his body.

Then Achilles raised his great war cry and thrust onward, all the Greek war-host behind him. Soon they were close before the city, and the Scaean Gate was choked with men and chariots, hunted and hunters. In that hour the Greeks might indeed have forced their way into Troy and the long siege might have been ended. But Paris stood in the gate-tower, fitting a new string to his bow, for the old one was frayed with much use. He chose an arrow from his quiver, leaned far out and took aim at Achilles in the crush that surged below.

The arrow flew on its way, and Apollo guided it so that it pitched deep into the battle-mass and, among all the trampling feet, found the target that it was meant for. It struck into Achilles' ankle in the unprotected place below the leg-guard, the place where his mother Thetis had held him when she dipped her babe in the river Styx. The one spot that the water had not touched and so could let death in.

He stumbled and fell, but rose again and wheeled round, shouting, "What coward has smitten me from afar? Let him come close and meet me with spear and sword!" And he dragged the arrow from the wound, letting loose a gush of blood.

There was blood everywhere. Darkness swam before his eyes. He staggered onward, striking blindly until his strength failed him and he came to a gasping halt, leaning on his spear. He gave a great hoarse shout. "Dogs of Troy! Dying though I am, you shall not escape my spears!" But with the words scarce out, he fell forward in the gateway, his armour clashing about him.

The Trojans stood and watched as hunters watch a dying lion, not daring to go near until the last breath is out of him. And so Hector's own dying words came true, that Achilles should meet his own death at the hands of Paris, in the Scaean Gate.

Then the Trojans in the gateway rushed forward to capture the body of Achilles in its glorious armour, while the Greeks struggled to bear it off to their camp for burial. Round his body the fight roared to and fro; men of both armies mingling together so thick that the archers on the ramparts dared not shoot for fear of slaying their own kind. At last Odysseus, though he was wounded in the knee, caught Achilles' wrists and heaved the body upon his back, and so went stumbling toward the ships. Ajax and his warriors followed behind to guard them, turning and charging into the midst of the Trojans whenever they came too near.

So, slowly, and fighting every step of the way, they carried dead Achilles back across the plain through the bodies of the slain to the black ships.

To his own hall they brought him, and there the women, Briseis first among them all, washed the blood and battle filth from his body, and laid him on a bier, spreading a white mantle over him. And they wept for him, lamenting and singing the death songs. And those who were left of the Greek leaders cut locks of their long hair for him, as he had cut his own for his friend Patroclus so short a time before.

Then up from the sea came his mother, Thetis of the Silver Feet, with all her maidens. They rose from the crystal chambers in the depth of the waters, moving up like the waves on a summer day, and their sweet sad singing echoed all along the shore. Then fear struck at the Greeks and they would have fled; but old Nestor steadied them, saying, "No need for fear.

It is his mother with her sea maidens come to look upon her dead son." And they stood firm once more.

And Thetis and the sea nymphs came and stood round him, and added their own sweet singing to the lamenting of the mortal women.

The Greeks built a great stack of wood and laid Achilles on it, with sacrificed oxen and jars of oil and wine and honey, and set fire to the whole. And when the pyre was burned out they gathered the white ashes of the hero, and mingled them with the ashes of Patroclus in the same two-handed golden cup brought out from his tomb. And over them they raised the grave-mound yet higher than it had been before, and set up a tall marker stone on its crest, that men passing by on land or out at sea would see it and remember who lay there.

Then they held the funeral games for him: chariot races and foot races, boxing and wrestling, as they had held them for Patroclus. And to all the winners Thetis gave rich and honourable prizes. Lastly, when the games were ended, she brought out her son's bright and splendid armour that Hephaestus had wrought for him and, laying it at the foot of the grave-mound, she said, "Let these arms be claimed as prize by the best and bravest of the warriors, by the one or the other of those two who saved Achilles' body out of the hands of the Trojans."

And so saying, she turned from them all and went

back to the sea, and her sea maidens with her.

Then Ajax and Odysseus stood up to claim Achilles' armour, both sure of their own worth, and both of them the bravest of the brave. And old Nestor stood up also, saying, "This is a grievous thing, that the best of the heroes left to us should contend for such a prize. For the loser will be sore at heart and may well feel that we have rejected him and he is not one of us as he was before; and so we shall suffer great loss. But if the thing must be, then let us not judge between them ourselves lest, one choosing Odysseus and another Ajax, bad blood should grow between us that way. There are many Trojan captives among us, waiting for their ransoms to be paid. Let the task of judgment be given to them."

"That is a wise word," said Agamemnon the High King. The captive Trojans were brought out and set in the midst of the assembly. And Odysseus and Ajax, standing before them, each spoke out his claim to the armour of Achilles. Ajax spoke first; but the god Dionysus, who always rejoiced in mischief-making, breathed a kind of drunkenness into him so that he spoke roughly and foolishly, not only making his own claim but seeking to belittle Odysseus by calling him a coward and a weakling.

When he had done, Odysseus said softly, "Let the Trojans judge whether I have earned the ugly names that Ajax has bestowed on me, remembering my many deeds in battle against them, and that it was I who carried off the Luck of Troy; remembering also that he did not find me so weak – though I had a newly healed wound on me – when we wrestled together at the funeral games for Patroclus."

Then the Trojan captives agreed among themselves that Odysseus was the greater of the two who stood before them, and awarded him the armour of Achilles.

And the dark blood flew to Ajax's face and he could speak no word, but stood rigid and unmoving, until his friends led him away to his own hall.

There he sat to the day's end and would not eat or drink or speak, for the dumb madness of the god that was in him. The madness was still with him when the dusk came down; and when the dusk had deepened into the dark, the evil thoughts came swirling yet more thickly in his head. He took his sword and rushed out into the night, making for the hall of Odysseus to hack him limb from limb.

But before he reached it, he came upon the flock of sheep which the Greeks kept for their meat, and he plunged into the fold, raging up and down and slaying blindly as he went, knowing nothing but the urge to kill.

And when the dawn came, his senses returned to him, and he saw that he had not slain Odysseus, but stood in a pool of blood with the hacked carcasses of dead sheep all about him.

He could not live with the disgrace of the madness that had come upon him. He fixed his bloody sword with its hilt set firmly in the ground, and drew back a little, then ran and fell forward upon the point that took him cleanly through the heart; and so made an end.

WHEN THE GREEKS found Ajax dead by his own hand, they lamented for him so that all the seashore was loud with their sorrow. And Odysseus said, "Would that the Trojans had not awarded me the armour of Achilles, for rather would I have lost it to Ajax, than that this more bitter loss should have come upon the whole war-host!"

And they burned and buried Ajax's body and lamented over him as they had lamented over Achilles.

They knew that, though they had slain Hector and defeated the Amazons and the dark army of Memnon, and had the Luck of Troy in their keeping, they had lost too many of their own champions and were no nearer to taking the city and Helen than they had been ten years ago.

So, near to despair, they went to Calchas their soothsayer, and begged him to tell them what to do. Calchas looked into the dark places within himself and listened to the voices that spoke there, and told them, "Fetch Philoctetes the archer from the island of Lemnos, for the word of the gods is that we shall not take Troy without his aid."

Now the Greeks had landed on Lemnos to take on fresh water on their way to Troy ten years before; and there one of their number, Philoctetes, had

118

fought a poisonous dragon who lived among the hills. The dragon had bitten him in the foot, and though he had killed it at last, the wound did not heal but dripped with venom and gave off a sickening stench. Philoctetes, in agony, kept the camp awake at night with his cries.

The Greeks had grieved for him, but could not bear to have him with them in the close quarters of a ship, and so had left him behind on the desolate isle when they sailed on their way. But now, late in the day, the gods were telling Calchas that they could not gain Troy without him. So Diomedes and Odysseus set sail to fetch him; and landing on the forsaken shore they heard his familiar cries of pain and despair, which guided them to a cave among the coastwise rocks.

And there they found him, piteous and terrible, worn to a skeleton with long matted hair and beard, and eyes sunk deep into his head. He lay moaning on a great pile of seabirds' feathers, his bow and arrows lying ready to his hand, and all the cave floor littered with the feathers and bones of the birds that he had shot for food; and his wounded foot still oozing with the stinking venom.

When he saw Odysseus and Diomedes coming, he seized his bow and fitted an arrow, dipped in his own poison, to the string. But they held up their hands in the sign that they came in peace, and he laid the bow down again and let them draw near. They sat on the rocks and told him the reason for their coming, and promised that if he came with them his wound should be tended and they would do all that they could to make amends for having deserted him. Philoctetes listened to them and at last said that he would return with them to Troy.

So the rowers laid him on a litter and carried him down to the ship. Odysseus bathed the wound with water warmed over a driftwood fire and poured oil into it and bound his foot with soft linen. They gave him supper and wine such as he had not tasted for ten years. And next morning they sailed for Troy.

Fair winds brought them swiftly to the shore where the black ships lay, and they carried him up to Agamemnon's hall, where the High King made him welcome and Machaon the healer did all that could be done for his foot. They gave him women slaves to tend him, and twenty well-broken horses, and vessels of fine bronze. They bathed him and cut and combed his hair, and gave him a robe from the king's own chest to replace his rags. And soon, feeling the strength coming back into him, he was eager to carry his bow into battle and send his arrows – he still had some that were poisoned – among the Trojans.

The Greeks thought it an ill thing to use venomed arrowheads, but Philoctetes said, "This is the skill that I have learned in ten long years. If now you would have my help, then you must have it in my way."

The next time the Greeks went up against the high walls of the city, and Paris on the ramparts was loosing his arrows down into the midst of them, Philoctetes saw him and cried out, mocking, "Very proud you must be of your archer's skill, and of your arrow that slew the great Achilles; yet I also have my skill, and the bow in my hands was drawn by the mighty Heracles himself!"

He set an arrow to the bowstring and drew and loosed all in one swift movement. The bowstring rang and the arrow sped on its way. It grazed the hand of Paris, no more, but within three heartbeats of time the poison was about its work. The bitter pain woke and grew and spread like fire within Paris, and with a cry he fell to the ground.

The Trojans carried him back into the city, and the physicians tended him all night long. But nothing eased his agony, and at dawn he cried out, "There is but one hope for me. Take me to the nymph Oenone who dwells at the foot of Mount Ida!"

Then his friends laid him on a litter, and carried him up through the steep woods by the path that he had followed so often when he was young and going to visit his love, but had not followed for many a long year. At last his bearers came to Oenone's cave, and smelled the sweet smoke of her cedar-wood fire, and heard the sad low notes of the song that she was singing.

Paris called to her, and she heard his voice and came out and stood in the cave entrance, pale as a moon moth against the firelit dark behind her. The bearers set the litter down at her feet, and Paris reached out to touch her knees, beseeching her mercy, but she drew back, gathering her robe closer round her.

"Lady," he pleaded, "do not hate me. Do not deny me so, for this pain is more than I can bear. Truly, it was not of my own free will that I left you lonely here, for the Fates themselves led me to Helen; and I wish that I had died in your arms before ever I saw her face! Have pity on me for the love that was once between us, and do not let me die in agony here at your feet!"

But Oenone answered him in a small cold voice, "It is over-long since you left me for the love of Helen. Surely she is fairer than I am, and better able to help you. Go back to her now and let her take away your pain."

And she turned and went back into the cave, and flung herself down weeping beside the fire. Yet in a while her heart softened, and she rose and went back to the cave entrance, thinking to find Paris still lying there. But with his last hope gone, he had bidden his bearers to carry him away into the dark of the forest, as a dying beast seeks the wild. And even as Oenone stood in her cave mouth, gazing about her for some sign of him, he was already dead.

His bearers carried his body swiftly down through the crowding oak woods, back to the city. And there his mother wailed for him, leading the other women in their keening, and Helen sang the death songs over him as she had done over Hector, remembering what had once been between them. The people raised a great pile of dry wood and laid his body on it, and set fire to the brushwood so that the flames leapt up through the darkness toward the sky.

Meanwhile, Oenone was roaming through the dark woods, crying and calling for her love like a lioness whose cubs the hunters have carried away. At last she saw the flames of the pyre far below her, and she knew their meaning all too well. Then she cried out that now Paris was all hers, and that though, living, he had left her for another love, in death they should be together and never parted any more. And she began to run — down through the steep oak woods, down through the thickets where the wood nymphs were wailing for him, out over the plain to where a great throng of Trojans was gathered about the blazing pyre.

She pulled her veil close over her head like a bride and, speeding through the crowd that parted to let her pass, she leapt upon the high-piled fire, into the very midst of it where the flame-tongues leapt as though to lick the stars, and flung herself down beside the body of Paris, clasping it in her arms.

So the fire took them both together; and when the flames died down, men gathered their mingled ashes into a golden cup, and set the cup in a stone chamber and piled the dark earth over all.

And long after, the wood nymphs planted two briar roses on the grave-mound which, as they grew, leaned to each other and plaited their arching sprays together, until they seemed not two, but one.

AFTER THE DEATH of Paris, Helen was still not given back to Menelaus, her true marriage-lord. Maybe the Trojans thought that it would be dishonourable, fearing that if they gave her back she would be put to some cruel death. So Deiphobus, one of Paris' remaining brothers, took her into his own house.

And still the war went on.

Soon the Greeks made another desperate assault on the city walls; but safe behind their battlements, the Trojans drove them back with hornet flights of arrows. In vain Philoctetes loosed his poisoned shafts against them; they fell back from the stone walls or lodged harmlessly in the timbers of the gates. And the Greeks who sought to climb over the defences were speared or crushed by the great stones flung down upon them.

At night they fell back to their ships. Agamemnon called together his council. Few enough were left of the leaders who had once come to that call. And as so often before, they turned to the wisdom of Calchas the soothsayer.

"Yesterday," said Calchas, standing in their midst, "I saw a hawk chasing a dove. She escaped from him and hid herself in a cranny in the rocks below the city walls. For a long while the hawk tried to follow her in, but he could not reach her. So he flew off a short distance and hid himself also among the rocks. Then, in a while, the poor foolish dove fluttered out into the sunlight; and the hawk stooped on her and killed her. Now therefore, let us learn from the hawk, and since by strength we can do nothing more against Troy, let us turn to cunning."

Then Athene planted in Odysseus' mind the seed of an idea: one of the cunning ideas for which he was famous. And he stood up and unfolded it to the listening Greeks.

Let them fashion a horse of wood: an enormous horse with a hollow body. And in the body let the bravest men of the war-host hide themselves, fully armed. Then let all the rest of the war-host go aboard their ships and sail as though for home, but go no further than the off-shore island of Tenedos, and lie hidden on the far side.

The Trojans would surely come out from the city, like Calchas' dove, to see if the Greek camp was really abandoned and to look at the great horse, wondering why it had been made and left there. And, lest they should look too closely, or do some harm to the beast and so discover the men within, let one of the Greeks – he must be clever and brave and yet one whom the Trojans did not know by sight – remain behind to be discovered by them. And being discovered, let him tell how the Greeks had given up all hope at last and sailed for home, but fearing that the lady Athene was angry with them for the theft of the Luck of Troy, they had built the great wooden horse as an offering to her, that she might not send storms against them on their homeward way.

If he could make them believe this story, like enough they would drag the horse into the city and set it up in her temple as a trophy of war. Then in the night the hidden war-band must come out and open the gates to their comrades, who would have returned from Tenedos as soon as the cloaking dark came down.

Calchas approved of this plan, and seeing two birds flying past on the right, which was a good omen, he declared that it would go well. Then Epeius the boxer, who was the best carpenter in all the war-host, gathered men to help him, and set about the task.

Next day half the war-host, with axes in their hands, went to fell trees in the woods that skirted Mount Ida. They felled oak and pine and maple, and harnessed mules to the trunks and hauled them down to the camp. Epeius and his men hewed the raw timber into planks and shaped pieces. In three days the gigantic horse was finished, its proud crest upreared taller than the roof ridge of Agamemnon's hall, and in its hollow belly dark space for a score of men.

Odysseus called for one man to remain behind and let himself fall into the hands of the Trojans, and a young warrior named Sinon stood up to answer the call. He had never been a front-fighter — if he had been, the Trojans would have known him – but many of the front-fighters would not have had his courage that day.

Nestor would have been the first to climb into the horse's belly, but he was too old and the rest would not let him. Agamemnon would have been the second, but he must sail with the fleet to Tenedos, and command the war-host when they returned. Menelaus climbed in, and Odysseus and Diomedes, Epeius the horse's builder himself, and many more.

Earlier, Menelaus had taken Odysseus aside, and told him that if they captured Troy (and now they must capture it, or die at the hands of the Trojans) he would give him one of his own cities, that they might always be near to each other. But Odysseus smiled and shook his head. He had no wish to leave his own harsh island kingdom of Ithaca. "But if we both live through this night, there is another gift that I may ask of you. One which will cost you neither land nor gold nor men in the giving."

Menelaus swore by the splendour of Zeus that whatever the gift might be, he would gladly give it, when the time came. And they went with their arms about each other's shoulders to put on their armour, and took up their cramped places in the belly of the horse.

The hidden war-band muffled themselves in thick cloaks, that their armour might not ring and clash to betray them as the horse was dragged along. And there they crouched in the dark, waiting, while outside the army fired the camp and launched their ships, and headed under oars and sail for the island of Tenedos.

From the walls of the citadel the Trojans saw the smoke of the burning camp billowing up into the sky, and the fleet putting out to sea. And their hearts lifted within them and they opened the gates and went down to the seashore. But they went fully armed in case of a trap, and they sent scouts ahead of them. They found the timber town burning and the whole camp deserted, and only the chocks and the keel-scars above the tide-line to tell where the ships had been. And they saw the great horse standing tall among the ruins, gleaming with the silken corn-stalk colour of new wood.

Priam and his nobles gazed at it, marvelling at its size and beauty, wondering what its purpose might be, and half afraid. And as they stood there Laocoon, the high priest of Poseidon, came hurrying down from the city, his two young sons and a great company of citizens with him.

While he was still far off he shouted to them in warning, "O my friends, leave that thing untouched! Do you think that the Greeks would leave us a gift without treachery in it? Either they have left men of their own shut within it, ready to come forth against us at the right time, or there is some evil magic in the creature itself to do us harm!"

And he flung the spear he carried at the horse's rounded belly. As it struck, there came a growling and a ringing from the hollow space within the timbers; and maybe the Trojans would have felt the danger and aided him to hack the thing open then and there. But at that same instant a knot of warriors came towards them, dragging Sinon in their midst.

They flung him at Priam's feet. "We found this hiding among the reeds," one of them said. "If we put fire to the soles of his feet, maybe he will tell us the secret of this wooden monster."

But Sinon let out a howl. "Was there ever a more miserable man than I? First my own people and now the Trojans both hate me to the death!"

"Tell us how you earned the hatred of your own people, and how you come to be here when they have gone, and it may be that we will cease to hate you," said the old king, and signed to his men to let the captive up.

"I will tell you what you ask, Lord King," said Sinon, drawing a deep breath to begin his story. "I was friend and armour-bearer to the chieftain Palamedes, whom the wicked Odysseus slew in secret for the hatred that he bore him. I was filled with wrath and had not the wisdom to hide it. I talked wildly, and my talk came to Odysseus' ears, so that he sought to slay me also. Then Calchas the soothsayer —" he broke off. "But what use to tell all the story, you will not believe it. Slay me, then; it is what Agamemnon and Odysseus desire.

Menelaus would thank you for my head."

That made the Trojans yet more curious, and Priam bade him to go on. So he told them, weeping and shuddering, that the Greeks had consulted an oracle as to their homeward voyage, and the oracle had bidden them to sacrifice one of their number to gain fair winds and calm seas. They had asked Calchas to choose the sacrifice, and Calchas had chosen him, Sinon. So he had been bound and held fast while the great horse which was their peace-offering to Athene was built, and he would have been dead by now if he had not managed to escape and hide among the reeds until the ships had sailed.

Sinon told his tale so well that the Trojans believed him and unbound his hands, rejoicing that the great horse threatened no harm to them, but was a peace-offering to Athene for the theft of the Palladium.

But they had scarcely done so when a terrible thing happened. Two great sea serpents appeared, heading out of the morning mists toward the shore, their crimson-crested heads upreared, their bodies snake-coiling through the water, lashing up the shallows and leaving behind them a wake like a thirty-oar galley. And before anyone could believe what they saw, let alone turn to run from the peril, they were plunging ashore, sea-flame flickering in their eyes, the forked tongues between their gaping jaws hissing and whiplashing to and fro.

They flew upon the two young sons of Laocoon, flinging their coils about them, and even as their father rushed to the rescue, it was too late. From the boys' mangled bodies they turned upon him. Before the horrified Trojans could so much as throw a spear, they flung their coils about him, tightening themselves about his throat and body, so that after one dreadful shriek that seemed to tear the skies apart, he could make no sound at all as the life was crushed out of him.

Then the serpents shook loose their coils and were gone, swifter than any flying spear could follow, across the plain and into the city. The priestesses in the temple of Athene saw them come, and saw them go across the marble pavement, to disappear behind the shield of the goddess' great statue and into some unknown lair behind her feet.

Priam and the rest of his company down by the shore stood as though stunned about the crushed and shapeless bodies of Laocoon and his sons. It seemed clear to them that the serpents were Athene's wrath against the priest for having cast his spear at her sacred horse; and if she was not to be made yet more angry, the enormous offering must be brought into the city and up to its rightful place in her temple.

They lashed ropes to the great horse, and laid rollers in front of it like men launching a ship, and took turns, Sinon among them, in long hauling-teams, to drag the thing rocking and lurching over the rough ground, across the plain and up to the Scaean Gate.

In the gateway people came running to meet them, and boys and maidens set their hands to the hempen ropes and helped to haul. Cassandra, the old king's daughter who had foreknowledge, cried out that the horse would be the death of Troy if they brought it within the gates. But no one listened to her.

With shouting and dancing and the singing of praise-hymns, the monster horse with its hidden load came lurching on up the last slope and over the rubble that the years of fighting had left there. On between the gate-towers and up the steep streets until it stood within the citadel, the high town, in the inner court of the great temple of Athene.

ALL DAY the people rejoiced, singing and dancing in the streets, decking their temples with branches of oak and myrtle in readiness for a sacred festival next day. And when all was done and darkness fell, they went to their own places and lay down to sleep.

By then, covered by the quiet darkness before moonrise, the fleet was returning from Tenedos as swiftly as the rowers could send their ships through the water. And crouched close in the airless space within the horse's belly, Odysseus and his fellows waited with straining ears and breath in check, while high on the temple wall Sinon strained his eyes seaward for the signal from the High King's ship, to tell him that the fleet was close in shore and the time had come to let out the hidden warriors. And all around, Troy lay quiet in sleep.

At last the signal came: a red blink of fire, far over in the darkness out to sea. Sinon's heart stumbled within him and began to race. He dropped from the wall and made his way to where the great horse stood, its shape blotted against the sky that was silvering towards moonrise. Standing beneath it, he cried out once, like a shore bird but not quite like a shore bird, to those listening within.

Then Epeius drew back the pine-wood bars, and

a trapdoor fell open in the horse's side. A rope came spooling down from it, and one by one the warriors, Menelaus and Odysseus and Diomedes and the rest, came dropping to the ground.

They stole down like armed shadows from the high place to the city gates. They slew the gate guards and flung open the broad gates to their fellow Greeks swarming up towards them. Then terror came upon sleeping Troy. The dark tide of warriors poured through and became a river of flame, as men kindled torches at the guardhouse fires and ran to burn the houses of the city.

Men, half-waking and half-armed, straggled out to meet them and were cut down. The night was full of the screams of women and children. The air grew thick with the sounds of battle, and fire went roaring through the city as it goes through a cornfield when a high wind is blowing.

But Odysseus had no part in all this. Indeed no man had seen him since the war-band came out from the horse's belly.

Diomedes, with Automedon and a growing band at his heels, had found the king's palace and overcome the guards in the outer court. They were flinging firebrands up on to the roofs, where defenders were tearing up the heavy coloured roof-tiles to hurl down upon them. Guarding their heads under their shields, they charged the main doors with war-axes and gilded beams torn from lesser buildings. The door-leaves burst open, tearing the bronze-sheathed hinge-posts from their sockets, and the men spilled through into the courts and chambers and colonnades beyond, cutting down the guards who stood against them.

No bolts or bars nor desperate courage of drawn swords could hold them back. They stormed up one passageway and down another, until they came at last to an inner court where stood an altar to the gods of the home, with an ancient bay tree bending over it as though to shield it from the fiery sky. And there the queen and the princesses had gathered, clinging about the twisted trunk like doves that have swooped to shelter from a storm. But there was no refuge for them, nor for Priam the aged king himself, who knelt praying to the gods before the altar.

A young warrior, drunk with fire and killing, seized him by his long white hair and dragged him backwards on the altar steps, and drove his sword through the old man's body so that his life-blood fouled the sanctuary where he had so often made offerings to the gods.

And they bound the royal women, despite all their screams and struggling, and dragged them captive away.

All through the city was fire and killing and the crashing down of walls and roofs as, after ten years' siege, mighty Troy was put to the sword.

But Helen had not been with the rest of the

royal women, and Menelaus had gone striding off through the palace courts where rags of burning timbers fell from the sky, seeking the house of Deiphobus, for he guessed that, with no other of the king's sons still living, that was where she would be.

He knew when he had found the right house, for in the entrance he came upon Deiphobus lying sprawled in his armour, the spear that had killed him standing upright in his breast. A chain of crimson footprints that started in the pool of his blood led on through the portico and into the darkness of the hall beyond.

Menelaus followed them like a hound on the scent; and so found Odysseus, leaning as though weary against one of the central pillars of the great chamber with the light of burning roofs glinting through the high windows upon his armour, and a trickle of his own blood oozing darkly out from his sleeve.

"Where is Helen?" Menelaus demanded, standing in the doorway, his sword naked in his hand. "If you are hiding her —"

Odysseus raised his head. "Earlier today you swore to give me the thing that I asked for. Whatever it might be."

"Ask then, and the thing is yours," Menelaus said. "I am not an oath breaker, though now is surely not the time —"

Odysseus said, "I ask for the life of Helen of the Fair Cheeks, that I may give it back to her in payment for my own life, which she saved for me when I came here seeking the Luck of Troy."

There was a long stillness in the great chamber, a hollow stillness amid all the outcry of the sacked city beyond the walls. Then Helen, with her pale robes gathered close about her, stole from the dark corner where she had been hiding. She fell at her lord's feet, her golden hair outflung all about her, and reached her hands beseechingly to touch his knees, with no word spoken.

Menelaus stood looking down at her, remembering that she had betrayed him to go with Paris, and left his hearth desolate and his child without a mother. And if it had not been for his promise to Odysseus he would have slain her in that moment. But he had made the promise, and because of it he held back.

As he still stood looking down at her, he began to remember other things from the time that they had shared together before Paris came. Pity and love stirred again in his heart. His drawn sword slipped from his grasp and fell ringing upon the pavement. He stooped and gathered her up, and her white arms went round his neck even as he coughed in the smoke of burning Troy.

When dawn came, Troy lay in ashes, the temple of Athene and the great horse with all the rest. The gold and silver, the ivory and amber were being shared among the Greek war-host. Priam lay dead before his household altar; the scorched bodies of his slain warriors lay piled in the fallen streets waiting for the dogs and the birds of prey. And the women were being herded to the ships of their new masters.

Hector's baby son lay dead beneath the ramparts from which he had been thrown in the fighting, as Andromache was thrust aboard the ship of a new prince of the Myrmidons. Princess Cassandra was carried to the great ship of Agamemnon himself. Only Helen, who, after Discord with her golden apple, had been the cause of it all, was led with honour, as a queen and not a slave, to the ship of her husband Menelaus.

The long siege was over, and in the young light of morning the ships of the great fleet were run down into the shallows. The rowers sprang aboard and took up their oars; and leaving the boat-strand empty save for the shore birds crying, and the smoke of Troy still rising behind them, they set their prows toward the home beaches that they had left so many years ago.

HOW TO PRONOUNCE THE GREEK NAMES

The letter *e* is pronounced long, as in "me", but when marked *ĕ* it is pronounced short, as in "wet".

The letters *i* and *y* are pronounced *ea* as in "bead", or *i* as in "bin".

The letters *eu* together are pronounced like the word "you".

The letters *au* together are pronounced *ow* as in "how".

The letters *ae, oe, ei* together are pronounced like the *e* in "me".

The letters *ch* are pronounced like *c*, as in "chord".

The letter *g* is pronounced like *j*, as in "giant".

The letters *rh* are pronounced like *r*, as in "rat".

The accent is on the syllable marked ´.

These are some of the more difficult pronunciations:
Achílles
Aegé-an
Aené-as
Agamémnon
Andrómache
Antílochus
Aphrodíte
Astýanax
Athéne

Aúlis

Autómĕdon

Brisé-is

Cálchas

Chíron

Chrysé-is

Dĕ-íphobus

Di-o-médes

ĕpeí-us

Eumélus

Eurýalus

Eurýpylus

Hecaméde

Hĕcuba

Hĕlĕnus

Hephaéstus

Héracles

Hippólyta

Idómĕneus

La-o-có-on

Lycomédes

Machá-on

Mĕnĕlá-us

Méri-ones

Mycénae (my-see-nee)

Mýrmidons (mer-midons)

Odýsseus

Oenóne

Palamédes

Patróclus

Péleus

Penthĕsilé-a

Philoctétes

Polýdamas

Poseídon

Protesilá-us

Rhésus

Sarpédon

Scaé-an

Styx (sticks)

Thersítes

Thrasymédes

Xánthus

Zeús

 # SOURCE BOOKS

Virgil's *The Aeneid*, translated by W.F. Jackson-Knight
(Penguin, 1956)

Dictionary of Greek and Roman Mythology,
by David Kravitz (New English Library, 1975)

Everyday Things in Homeric Greece,
by C.H.B. Quennell (Batsford, 1928)

The Greek Myths, by Robert Graves (Penguin, 1955)

Introduction to Homer's *The Iliad*,
translated by Martin Hammond (Penguin, 1987)

The Myths of Greece and Rome,
by H.A. Guerber (Harrap, 1942)

In Search of the Trojan War,
by Michael Wood (BBC Books, 1985)

*The Western Way of War: Infantry Battle in Classical
Greece*, by V.D. Hanson (Oxford University Press, 1991)

ROSEMARY SUTCLIFF
is widely regarded as one of the finest
children's writers of the twentieth century,
with over 50 books to her name. Her novel
The Lantern Bearers won the Carnegie Medal in
1959, while *The Eagle of the Ninth* (1954),
The Shield Ring (1956), *The Silver Branch* (1957),
Warrior Scarlet (1958) and *Tristan and Iseult*
(1971) have all received Carnegie Medal
Commendations. In 1978, *Song for a Dark Queen*
won the Children's Rights Workshop "Other"
Award. She received the U.S. Libraries Phoenix
Award in 1985 and was honoured with the O.B.E.
in 1975, followed by the C.B.E. in 1992,
for services to children's literature.
Her death in 1992 was a sad loss to readers
throughout the world.

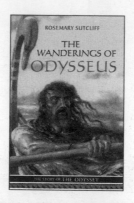

THE WANDERINGS OF ODYSSEUS
The Story of THE ODYSSEY

Rosemary Sutcliff

The siege of Troy is ended. The city is in ruins
and the Greeks can finally return home victorious.
But for Odysseus, King of Ithaca, another long test
of courage, endurance and cunning is just
beginning. Buffeted by ill winds into unknown
seas, Odysseus and his crew find themselves
confronted by a terrifying Cyclops, then trapped
by the enchantments of Circe, then facing the
deadly temptations of the Sirens and the perils of
Scylla and Charybdis. Meanwhile, Odysseus's wife,
Penelope, is besieged by suitors laying claim
to her husband's throne.